Legacy of Love

by *Patty Rosvall*

NEW BEGINNINGS
Salt Lake City, Utah

ACKNOWLEDGEMENTS

Many people need to be thanked

for their work and encouragement

on this project.

I could not have done it without

the gifts of love from my mother,

Steve Rigby, Hazel Rimmasch,

and Jan Snow.

Legacy of Love
©1997 by Patty Rosvall
All rights reserved.
Printed in the United States of America.
No portion of this book may be reproduced in any form
without written permission from the publisher,
New Beginnings, Salt Lake City Utah.
Library of Congress Catalog Card Number: 97-67061

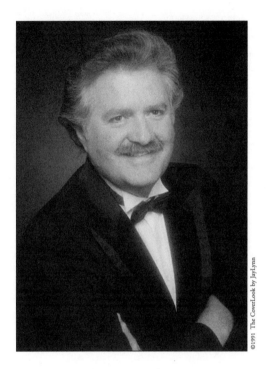

This book is dedicated to Gene,
my husband of twenty-five years,
my mentor and friend,
who taught me the meaning of joy.
My life is blessed to have
known him.

"To everything there is a season,
and a time to every purpose under heaven;

"A time to be born, and a time to die;
a time to plant, and a time to pluck up that which
is planted;

"A time to kill, and a time to heal,
a time to break down, and a time to build up;

"A time to weep, and a time to laugh;
a time to mourn, and a time to dance;

"A time to cast away stones, and a time to gather
stones together; A time to embrace, and a time to
refrain from embracing;

"A time to get and a time to lose;
a time to keep, and a time to cast away;

"A time to rend, and a time to sew;
A time to keep silence, and a time to speak;

"A time to love, and a time to hate;
a time of war, and a time of peace."

ECCLESIASTES 3:1-8

CONTENTS

"A million times we have needed you;
A million tears we have cried,
If love, alone, could have saved you,
You never would have died.

"In life we loved you dearly;
In death we love you still.
Within our hearts you hold a place
No one else can ever fulfill.

"It broke our hearts to lose you,
But, you didn't go alone,
For part of us went with you
The day God took you home."

AUTHOR UNKNOWN

INTRODUCTION

My husband developed a sudden, severe, and rare illness which took him out of mortality in just sixteen days. All this time he lay comatose in the intensive care unit of a local hospital. I kept a daily diary of what transpired. This book is taken from those pages, as well as from the journal I have kept since.

Obviously, not everything could be included here. But, it is hoped that enough information has been given to make this story complete. Everything stated is true, to the best of my knowledge.

I hope anyone who reads these pages will find comfort in knowing there is a Father in Heaven who knows each one of us as an individual, who knows our needs better than we do, who loves each of us individually, and who answers our prayers.

I have come to know my Heavenly Father more than ever before in my life. I am so grateful for my eternal marriage in the House of the Lord, and I pray fervently that I will live the rest of my days worthy to be reunited with Gene forever in the life to come.

I don't understand fully about death, and why Gene had to be taken at a relatively early age. But I have learned that I don't have to understand everything. I only need to walk by faith.

Nor do I fully understand why my life was spared. But, I do know that to be of any value, my life needs to reflect the pure love of Christ. It is my desire to become an instrument in His hands to bring comfort, love, charity, and peace wherever I go.

This book is not so much a story about death, as it is about love. It is the story of a poignant love my husband and I shared for nearly a quarter of a century. As a newlywed, I used to think that he was one in a million. As the years passed. I began to realize I was wrong. He was one of a kind. This book was written as a legacy of love to my husband and best friend. It is a story I now want to share with you.

Part One

SHOCK

CHAPTER ONE

MARCH 5, 1995

"Blood pressure, 128/82.
Temperature, 98.8.
Pulse, 68.
Respiration, 18.
Vital signs are normal," documented the E.R. Nurse.

"Let's do some lab work," commanded the physician. "Let's do blood channels, urinalysis, chest x-ray, CT scan, blood cultures, and a lumbar puncture to see what we're dealing with."

Gene, my husband of twenty-five years—that is, twenty-four years and eleven months, had been admitted to the emergency room. He had become vacant, stuporous, and mostly unresponsive during the past four to five hours.

My husky neighbor and his strapping teenage son were able to help me get Gene to the hospital, at which time, he could barely shuffle into a wheel-chair.

By the time he was in the examining room, he was mostly comatose. All lab work was coming back normal, which was frustrating to the medical team and family alike.

Why was he in a coma? What was happening? Over the next four hours stroke had been ruled out. Gene was responding only to pain, but only through body language, not verbally.

Finally, he was admitted into ICU in the wee hours of the morning of March 6, 1995. The internist on call had to get out of bed and drive several miles to the hospital to attend to Gene. He was puzzled by the results of the tests, but was to remain as his primary care physician.

My recently married daughter, Jennifer, and I returned to our homes about 2:30 A.M., but sleep eluded us.

I remembered the events leading up to the time we were married. It was an interesting courtship. We both had an unspoken understanding that we would be married to each other. There had been no proposal from either of us to the other. Our love for each other had just been a continuation of ourselves.

MARCH 6, 1995

In returning to the hospital that morning, I could see that Gene's condition had worsened. He was even more comatose, although his neurological reflexes were still good. Heavy, rapid breathing, groaning, rapid heart rate, rapid respiration, and tremors in all four extremities were nonstop. His blood pressure and temperature readings vacillated. Profuse sweating drenched his body and hospital gown.

More blood gases were drawn. More blood tests were taken. Another lumbar puncture, an MRI and EEG were performed—again, with mostly normal results, except for some suspicious minute specks showing up in the MRI.

Gene was put on antiviral, antibacterial, and antiseizure IV medication. He was given oxygen per nasal canula. Although he wasn't seizing, his pronounced tremors persisted.

I could recall the time Gene had taken our two sons on a fishing excursion. He told them to stand on the bridge and cast their fishing lines down below the bridge, assuring them that fishes could always be found under bridges.

Moments later, Gene would be under the bridge, affixing fish he had caught onto the boys fishing hooks and then giving their lines a tug. The boys were so excited to each reel in the fish he had "caught."

MARCH 7, 1995

On this day Gene's condition remained unchanged. His breathing was rapid and labored. He was perspiring profusely. His rapid heart rate, groaning, and tremors persisted. His blood pressure readings and temperature readings had increased. However, his fists, which had been tightly clenched and drawn inward, had finally unclenched.

Gene had undergone arthroscopic knee surgery just forty-eight hours prior to his comatose condition. He was in excellent health and had come through the cartilage trimming very well. So what had brought this about?

It became suspected that what he had was some sort of toxic reaction which would just have to work itself out of his system.

In the meantime, more blood work, more blood gases, and more blood cultures were taken. Oxygen was increased to 4 liters. Another MRI was taken, this time to examine the cerebral-vascular network of the brain.

Later in the day, Gene seemed more relaxed, and his tremors were less exaggerated. But, he became very feverish and had to be given an ice bath. His breathing became less labored, and the groaning less frequent and less severe.

That evening brought more encouraging changes. Gene had closed his mouth and was breathing through his nose for the first time since his admittance. He appeared calmer and much more relaxed. In fact, he experienced no tremors for nearly thirty minutes.

Gene had a sense of humor and was always making me laugh. He could pass pundits with the best. People would phone him when they wanted to feel better. He could make me laugh so hard when I was angry, that I would really get disgusted with myself for not being able

*to stay angry. The fact was, I was a wimp in the presence
of a master humorist.*

MARCH 8, 1995

There was a calendar hanging on the wall of Gene's room.
For some reason I found it necessary to rip off the daily pages.
That morning he was still in a coma and breathing very rapid-
ly, and gasping for every breath. They finally placed a face
mask on him for oxygen, and set it for 60%, which is a poten-
tially dangerous level, but the monitor showed only an 89%
oxygen content in his blood. They brought a large fan into the
room to blow directly on Gene and had to give him Tylenol
for spiking fevers and sweats.

Gene was struggling for every breath, so much so, that he
made his oxygen mask squeak with each inspiration. They
came to draw blood gases again, and Gene tried unsuccessful-
ly to pull away from the pain.

Our two families had been in to visit every day, and the
bishop had come in to visit every day.

The internist decided Gene needed to be receiving some
nourishment, so they had to insert a nasogastric tube, which
was most unpleasant. They also had to do a small surgical procedure on the right forearm to insert a catheter into the superior vena cava for antibiotics. The antibiotics which were
being administered through the regular IV line had ruptured
his veins, and the superior vena cava (SVC) was a much larg-
er vein and could tolerate the medication better.

That evening Gene became agitated and restless. The continually blowing fan made me wish I could curl up in a huge blanket, yet Gene continued to be feverish and diaphoretic.

The change of shifts brought a new nurse to care for him. She was a real sweetheart. Actually, they all were. She washed his back, changed his soaked sheets, changed his body position, and placed "booties" over his toes to keep them warm while the fan was blowing. She also started his food supplement down the nasogastric (NG) tube. Robert, our son, decided it was an "all you can eat buffet."

"At times, Darling, you become so agitated that I become frustrated at my complete helplessness. I can only imagine how frustrated you are. There are times I wish so hard that you could communicate with me to tell me how I can make you more comfortable, and to tell me where you are hurting. I wonder so often if you are experiencing pain, because you groan so much."

The doctors had a research team trying to identify the problem they were dealing with. By that time, they had also ruled out meningitis and encephalitis because his blood cultures had come back negative. However, the second MRI showed some inflammation in the brain, from what, no one knew.

I knew he was about as dead as anyone could possibly be, and still be alive. When I went home that night, I tried to sleep, but could only mull over in my mind everything the doctors had told me, trying to make sense of it all.

I finally called my Relief Society president at 11:00 P.M.

She immediately, even at that hour, instigated a ward fast in Gene's behalf.

The first date our daughter had with her husband-to-be was fun for Gene, a practical jokester, and me. Upon finding out they were going to a local restaurant, we headed there, too. We asked the hostess if we might be seated next to a certain table (where our daughter and her date were talking animatedly). When she saw us being seated next to their table, she glowered at us. We kept pulling funny faces in return. For every disgusted glance in our direction, we gave a clown face back.

We left before they did, so we could place an "I love you" note on their windshield. When they got ready to leave, their waitress informed them that their meal had been paid for by the couple seated next to them. That was so much fun.

MARCH 9, 1995

I didn't know why, but I felt I had a morbid duty to tear the daily sheets off the wall calendar. I knew that if Gene didn't make a turn-around today, we would lose him.

The night nurse gave me a report of his status during the night. She told me he had seemed calmer and more relaxed; in fact, his tremors had subsided altogether. Breathing had been less labored and oxygen had been turned down to 50%. He only became agitated whenever anyone physically did something to him. However, he was still posturing with hands and feet clenched inward.

The bishop came in that morning to give him a blessing to correspond with the ward and family fast.

Later in the day, as I sat there watching him, Gene's agitation and fever increased. I wondered if it was because he knew I was there and was thus, trying to telepathize a message to me. Was my lack of response the thing that was agitating him?

The fan was still blowing twenty-four hours a day, yet he was still perspiring profusely.

A pulmonary specialist was called onto the case. Because Gene was breathing so hard, just heaving his body and gasping for every breath, it was decided to put him on a ventilator to help him breathe.

Through another small, surgical procedure, they also installed an arterial line to measure blood gases, monitor blood pressure, heart rate, etc. They were also able to take certain types of blood samples through it, so they didn't have to poke him as much.

Gene, being a practical joker, had a great time one particular Halloween. Our creative son-in-law had decorated a room in one of the local haunted houses for charity. Having a wolfman costume, Gene decided to have some fun. Arranging in advance, he became part of the decor in our son-in-law's room, scaring the daylights out of people. As a 48 year old at the time, he must have been going through his second childhood.

MARCH 10, 1995

Gene appeared much calmer today. His fingers and toes were much more relaxed. Last night, an infectious disease specialist was called in to review the case. He suggested Gene might be having an allergic response to something and probably needed to be placed on antiinflammatory medication.

"Now," I thought, "we're getting somewhere."

Frustratingly, twelve hours after the steroid medication had been started, Gene's condition remained unchanged. Allergic reactions generally always respond for the better following twelve hours of antiinflammatory medication.

I needed to be positive. So, on the positive side, Gene was not worse. In fact, oxygen had been turned down to 40%, and he was ventilating very well.

Another amazing thing happened today. The physicians finally arrived at a diagnosis—five days following his admission. It was called Acute Disseminated Encephalomyelitis, or ADEM, for short. ADEM, I learned, is an autoimmune disorder which destroys certain proteins in the central nervous system along the myelin sheath. It isn't viral in nature, but always follows a viral infection by ten to twenty days. What viral infection he may have had was unclear.

The doctors told me the prognosis for ADEM is very poor, meaning death. Or, if there was recovery, there may be permanent residual effects, depending upon which part of the central nervous system would be affected. In Gene's case, that involved the motor areas.

ADEM is rare and is hardly ever seen anymore. It used to be more common before the discovery of the measles vaccine. Sometimes children who contracted measles, a viral disease, would come down with ADEM. It has mostly affected children and young adults. Gene was the oldest person known to have contracted this condition.

One can only surmise that it wasn't very easy to determine a diagnosis. Gene's case became the talk of the entire medical community. His chart was faxed to the University Hospital to see what their experts could surmise. If Gene had been conscious, he may have thought he was pretty special to have contracted something so exotic. Well, he was special, but not for that reason!

All hospital personnel treated him with such kindness. Ever so many people were concerned about him. They kept the television on for him during the nights when I wasn't there, just to keep him company—in case he could still hear.

Tremors persisted, as did spiking fevers. However, Gene began to retain fluid in his tissues. After they had given him a diuretic, his urine ran like a faucet through the Foley catheter. It was comforting to know his kidneys still functioned.

Physical Therapy began to give him range of motion exercises twice a day. They asked me to bring in some cotton socks and high top shoes to help align his feet and prevent them from contracting inward.

An x-ray they took today showed a possible lung infection. They also treated him with heparin to keep his blood thin, thus reducing the chance of clotting while in his immobile state.

The respiratory therapist examined him and told me his lung capacity was actually a bit improved over the previous day, in spite of what the x-ray showed.

A special bed came in for Gene today. It had an air mattress which vibrated and or changed his body position from time to time in order to reduce the possibility of bedsores and blood clots. But every time the bed moved his body position, he got agitated and his blood pressure skyrocketed.

On the positive side: fingers and toes were more flaccid, pulmonary function was a bit improved, oxygen was down to 40%, knee and wrist joints were more relaxed, and respiratory rates had decreased from the high 50's to the low 20's by the time I left my sweetheart for the night.

Being on the executive board of our local teacher's association, Gene would have to take a business trip once or twice a year. I never looked forward to being alone during these times, so I would go shopping to lift my spirits. Gene would always leave me extra spending money for these shopping sprees. Sometimes I would spend more than he gave me, but he was always good natured about it and enjoyed seeing my newly purchased treasures.

On one of Gene's three-day trips, I saw a particular piece of furniture which I fell in love with and knew exactly where in our home it would be placed. It happened to be on sale, so I was delighted. When Gene returned home, I informed him I had saved him nearly one hundred dollars. Laughingly, he asked, "And just how much did that incredible savings cost me?"

MARCH 11, 1995

"Well, Darling, today is a new day in which to get better. How much can you improve today? Your doctors came in today and told me the neurological center at the University Hospital confirmed your diagnosis of ADEM and stated it was the worst case they had ever reviewed.

"You stubborn, gentle giant. When you 'fell,' you fell hard, resulting in such a quaking that it was felt all over this valley. People from all over this valley are praying for you, fasting for you, and pulling for you. Many different religions are holding prayer circles for you. It's been amazing to me."

The doctors increased his heparin today, and they also had to give him insulin for drug-induced diabetes. The massive doses of steroids they had been giving him as antiinflammatory agents had made his blood sugar levels skyrocket. They also determined that his temperature kept spiking because the part of his brain which regulated the thermostat had been affected by this atrocious condition.

It was becoming more evident, to me, that the anesthesia he had received for his arthroscopic knee surgery was the culprit. It had literally "fried" his brain.

Gene's nurse today was super. They all were. Sitting with Gene nearly twelve hours a day had allowed me to realize two things: (1) It had given me time to deal with my frayed emotions and some-what pull myself together; and, (2) It had allowed me to witness the care he was being given. Therefore, I had become very confident in his extraordinarily wonderful nursing care in the ICU. I began to feel more confident about leaving him to their competent care while I returned back to work.

On the positive side: Knees remained flexed today, instead of rigid and extended as in days past. Elbows and wrists were also more relaxed. Tremors had been very slight and lasted only minutes instead of hours. Breathing was not as labored. The physical therapist finally got his knee and ankle joints to bend to 90 degrees, a first, as they had been fairly "frozen."

> *After our daughter's marriage, there were some pretty lean times while they were struggling to finish college, work, and also have a nighttime cleaning job. Gene would often buy an extra few bags or boxes of groceries and secretly drop them off at their place while they were at work. Of course, they always knew who the bounty came from, and would always let us know that it was appreciated at a time when they were "destitute." Gene always had an uncanny sense which allowed him to help others when they needed it the most.*

MARCH 12, 1995

"Good morning, Darling. Today is the one-week mark.

You are receiving such wonderful care. Each day I come into your room I wish 'today's' nurse could be your permanent one. But then, the next day, I wish the same thing again with your new nurse. They have all been excellent."

Some positive things happened today. Gene's coloring was great. The puffiness in his tissues was completely gone. His posturing was about 80% improved. He was oxygenating well. But, his blood pressure still accelerated whenever he was being bothered, and his heart rate still raced at an average of 112 beats per minute. Oxygen was turned back up to 50%. Still, he seemed to have a lot of vitality.

In my prayers this morning, the thought came into my mind that I should stop being so concerned with things of the flesh, which are the normal and natural frailties of mortality. It came into my mind that I should be more concerned with the things of the spirit, because the spirit is everlasting, and the flesh is not.

I was feeling so positive that Gene was going to pull through.

The physical therapist was in again today. She was a petite little thing. It was almost comical how she had to go about giving his six-foot three inch frame range of motion exercises.

When the bishop came in today, he gave Gene another blessing to coincide with another ward fast. The one they held the first time was for him to be healed. The ward had asked me if they could hold another fast for him. I agreed, but on the condition that this time, everyone was to fast that the Lord's will would be done.

When the bishop came to visit and to bless Gene, he related to me what had happened in church that day. In Sacrament Meeting he had announced that anyone who had been fasting for Gene and who wanted to participate in a prayer circle for him, could meet in the Relief Society room following the meeting block. However, when they met for prayer, the Relief Society room had become so packed with well-wishers, they had to change the prayer circle to the chapel. He said that the chapel was so full, there were many who had to stand. If wishes alone could have made him well, he would have been out of the hospital by now.

"Well, goodnight, my darling. I feel comfortable leaving you in the hands of the professionals."

When Jennifer and her husband were first married, they cleaned doctors' offices in the evenings to help their financial situation. Interestingly, their good health waned during the time they had this extra responsibility. From time to time, one or the other of them would be too ill to help the other do the cleaning. There were many occasions when one or the other would phone us late at night, after we had gone to bed, requesting help because their mate was ill. Each time this occurred, Gene insisted I remain in bed while he got dressed and went out in the cold, dark night to help out—and never complained.

MARCH 13, 1995

"Hello again, my darling. Today is day eight. I had such a calm, peaceful feeling yesterday, but I confess, today I've been bawling my eyes out. I'm realizing more and more how very much I've depended upon you for everything, and I do mean everything—not only around the house, but for my day-to-day sanity, as well as my emotional comfort and strength. I have always thought of myself as being fairly independent, but now reality is forcing me into accepting how very much I love you and need you.

"I also realize how one-sided our love affair has been. You have given me all you have, indeed, your very life, while I have been the selfish recipient. If you live, I can promise you, with full conviction, that I'll never take you for granted again. You deserve so much more than I have given. I'm not making a bargaining promise, I'm making a genuine commitment to be the wife you deserve."

Today Gene's condition was unchanged, except that his liver enzymes were elevated, and his eyes were not tracking anymore. They told me that one eyeball was rolled up and the other one was off to the side; however, they didn't look that way to me when I opened his eyelids and looked at his sweet brown eyes.

I needed to be positive again. His blood pressure was good and was remaining stable. He didn't become agitated when the bed vibrated or changed his position. On the other hand, I didn't know if that was a positive sign, or if he was just giving up.

"You've fought so hard for so long, my valiant, gentle giant. I can hardly see what I'm writing because of the tears in my eyes.

"How can two people live and love together for 25 years and not feel a complete, devastating loss? You do remember that we have our Silver Wedding Anniversary in three weeks, don't you? Come back to me, Darling. Live! Live!

"If you die, I want to die, too. But I realize my journey hasn't come to its end. That's what is so sad! I want to be with you, even in death. You know I've always loved being with you! That's how it's been for 25 years, isn't it?"

Gene and I had done everything together—from yard work to house work, from doing laundry to preparing meals and doing the dishes, from grocery shopping to running errands, from studying to playing games. We had always been each other's best friend.

"I watched while the physical therapist was working with you, and as I followed every curve and line of your sweet body, I was reminded of how much I loved everything about you.

"You now have gigantic black blisters on the soles of your feet, where the high top shoes have forced your feet into proper alignment against their will. The shoes are now cast aside so your skin can heal.

"You just lie there so unresponsive and so near death. If I could give you my life, I would in a breath. When your respirations get down to five or six, as they are now, it worries me. I am still struggling for you and willing you to live."

I brought in some of his favorite audio tapes for him to listen to, provided he could still hear. I also brought in some of his after shave cologne for him to smell (a little aroma therapy).

I had been thinking that it was no small coincidence that I finally went back to school to get my degree, and that I had secured a stable job as a biology teacher. I also guessed that it was no small coincidence that Gene bought me a beautiful home four years ago, in an exceptionally wonderful ward, surrounded by caring neighbors.

"I'll go back to school in a couple of days, out of financial necessity, but my heart and soul, and very being, want to lie down next to you and die with you, or live with you—especially live with you! Oh, my darling, I don't know how my heart can go on beating when it is breaking—no, shattering into a million pieces."

On the positive side: They discontinued his antibiotics because they were assured the source of the problem was not infectious. His temperature remained below 100 degrees all day, without Tylenol. His heart rate was below 100 beats per minute all day. Respirations had been below 20 per minute all day. He was oxygenating well, at 96%—wow! His blood pressure remained stable.

There were four boys in Gene's family, and his father taught each of them to hunt and to fish. Soon after we were married, the men went on their annual pilgrimage to the mountains to play their hunting games. Gene was so distraught after killing a deer that he sold his rifle and became an animal advocate, even cutting down on his intake of meat.

He came to believe that animals were God's creatures and that it was man's responsibility to respect the lives of all of God's creations. He believed that animals were placed here for the benefit of man, and not to satisfy his ego.

MARCH 14, 1995

"Good morning, Darling. I was feeling quite glum yesterday, but after a long talk with Heavenly Father last night, I'm feeling a bit better. There are so many people who are absolutely convinced you're going to get well, that it's hard to not be convinced myself.

"Your doctor explained to me that the puffiness you've been having is normal for a comatose person. He told me all about capillaries seeping fluid when they're not exercised, and how reduced protein in the diet can also cause capillaries to seep fluid into the tissues.

"It's so cool in your room. I'm layered and freezing, but the constant blowing of the fan seems to help keep your temperature down. You've been doing so well. Your temperature is down to 99 degrees right now, and has been all night, without Tylenol. That's fantastic!

"Your heart rate is still below 100. Oxygen is set at 55%, and you're oxygenating well. Your blood pressure is remaining stable. However, you're being plagued with incessant hiccoughs. Some of this is due to your medication, but they are also partly caused by the insult your brain has sustained.

"Your knees are flexed, and your foot position is looking good, but your elbows are locked again. Overall, you're not worse. We just have to wait for your brain to heal. And it will!

"The sun is shining today, and as I look over this valley from your fourth floor window, I see patches of green breaking through a field of brown, barren trees. Nature is reawakening. My fervent hope is that you'll soon be awakening, too.

"You are keeping your head aligned today by yourself, without towels to prop it up. Until today, your head has flopped over to one side, and has had to be propped up with towels to reduce the chances of a kinked neck. You also seem more alert today. I know the CT scan they have scheduled for you is going to show improvement."

As Gene was wheeled back into his room following the CT scan, I was told he tolerated it very well. His vital signs were still stable, and his temperature was finally normal. This was the very best he had been in nine days.

One student teacher who was training under Gene's guidance told me a story about Gene I hadn't known. During lunch one day, in the faculty room, a female colleague was rummaging through her purse looking for an elusive dollar bill, stating over and over she knew it was there. She had wanted to buy a drink from the vending machine, but unable to find the dollar, she went over to the sink to get a drink of water.

Seeing that she had left her purse opened on the table in front of Gene, he slipped a dollar from his pocket into her purse. When the teacher returned to retrieve her purse, she saw the dollar bill and exclaimed, "I knew I had a dollar in here," and was able to purchase her drink afterall. He was always a quiet observer, never wanting anyone to know of his deeds for others.

MARCH 15,

"This is day ten. I had a real bad night last night, because I knew I had to talk with your doctors today about your medications. So, I have taken another day off from work and have sat beside you since 7:00 this morning in order to see all of them.

"I firmly believe you're having adverse reactions to the steroids they're giving you for inflammation, which has been seven times the therapeutic dose. Your doctors still want to continue with them. I don't, and my rationale is threefold: (1) The article about ADEM I was given to read said steroids don't help. (2) The results of yesterday's CT scan showed no improvement, so the steroids don't seem to be helping. (3) You are experiencing terrible side-effects.

"We reached a compromise. They have promised to taper them off over the next five days. So today, they cut your dose down to two times the therapeutic dose."

Some of the things which were happening, as stated in the Physician's Desk Reference as side-effects of high doses of steroids, were edema (fluid retention), petechiae (hundreds of tiny purple specks from broken capillaries), arrhythmias (irregular heart beats), hiccoughs, and diaphoresis (sweating).

Other possible side effects were intraocular pressure, perhaps leading to glaucoma and blindness. Gene's eyeballs seemed to be bulging under his eyelids lately. I just couldn't see him recover, only to be blind. I asked his internist to call in an ophthalmologist, but he assured me it wasn't necessary, in his opinion. Another side-effect could be increased intracranial pressure—just what we didn't need!

Last night his NG tube came out. When it did, he coughed up blood. Apparently, irritation from the feeding tube had caused a bleeding ulcer in his stomach. This resulted in another tube having to be inserted down his nose and into his stomach to pump out the blood. They had to reposition the feeding tube farther down, to give the ulcer a rest.

Another problem was that his bowels no longer had any bowel sounds. As a result, unkind tactics had to be implemented to get them moving again.

I had to sign for another surgical procedure in order to have something called a quad lumen inserted into his superior vena cava. The little NG tube just wasn't getting enough nourishment into his gigantic frame, so they had to also feed him through his SVC.

"They assured me, Dearheart, that they will be able to draw blood samples and give all your IV meds through the quad lumen. This will give your poor, bruised arm a needed rest."

Yet another surgical procedure they had me sign for today was to implant a new arterial line into his other forearm, as the one in his right arm was presenting serious problems.

Following the procedures, he was resting peacefully. His temperature had been normal for two days. He has been keeping his head aligned, as well as his feet and hands. His groaning had subsided, and he didn't appear to be in any pain.

"I brought in an audio tape for you to listen to today. It is the recording you made when your elementary school chorus performed two weeks ago, with you as their trainer and director. Do you remember it? I hope it brings you pleasure. Right now I'm playing a recording of the Tabernacle Choir for you. It's the tape you had recently purchased for your car. Do you remember when we sang at our Regional Conference four weeks ago, and we sat in the choir seats at the Tabernacle? It reminded us of when your mom sang with the Tabernacle Choir for thirty-two years.

"The sun sets every night as I sit here watching you, and my mood sinks with each sunset. I go home to a dark house, and it seems fitting for my mood. Our king-size bed is so lonely without you.

"This afternoon, I took a break and took care of some business. I was reminded again of all the things you do for us. I've taken such advantage of you, and can't understand why I haven't waited on you as much as you have me.

"Do you remember the nutrition stakes we bought for our ailing globe willow tree which we planted four years ago at our new home? I hammered them into the ground around the tree today. You would have done that. I'm determined to save that tree, even though the tree surgeon says it's probably hopeless. Maybe it is hopeless, but it is a part of you and me. And right now I have a real need to hang onto it and do whatever I can to make it live. I water it faithfully, and spray the fungal infestation with the Clorox mixture, just as we did in the fall.

"They just gave you a dose of ulcer medication to help coat your stomach, due to your newly developed ulcer.

"I finally found your checkbooks today. I'm trying to figure out your bank accounts. You never did balance your bank statements, but you always seemed to know exactly how much you had as a balance, and never, ever, bounced a check. I'm still looking for your special savings account which has the funds in it to cover our IRS audit. I wish I knew the name of the lady at the IRS office with whom you were working, so I could phone her to find out the status of our audit. These are the things you always took care of.

"I took your car for a little drive today. Tootsie (our dog) loved getting out for a change, as I've been neglecting her lately. Your darned car is so big for me. I have to sit on a pillow to see over the hood. That's what happens when I marry a giant—a gentle giant.

"Robert is insisting on taking me and Jenny out for dinner tonight. I realize it is his way of coping with a feeling of helplessness, but I want to be in only two places: here with you, or home with my memories of you.

"On the positive side: Some of your side-effects are lessening since they lowered your steroid medication. I love you, Darling. Goodnight."

Gene's teaching colleagues would tell me of the times he would daily teach his students they had worth. He would also take advantage of situations when he would give instruction in moral values.

One day at recess, a fight broke out between a couple of his students. He gave them loving instruction rather than punishment. He asked them if they knew what it meant to deal from strength. Gleaning their answers and networking them into his lesson, Gene instructed them, "Don't let hate consume you. When you do, you are no longer the boss. You let hate become your boss. Everyone has a weak side to them and a strong side to them. When you draw from your strong side, you are dealing with strength."

MARCH 16, 1995

"Well, Dear, this is day eleven. Your vital signs are still stable, and your urine output is good. In fact, your intake and output are exactly equal, which is quite unusual. Your color looks great. You seem a bit more reactive to stimuli today, which could be good or bad. You're oxygenating well.

"They had to infuse you with platelets today, as your platelet level became dangerously low. They also discontinued your antiviral medication today, as they are certain you don't have a virus. What you have cannot be transmitted to others, neither did you contract it from anyone. I am convinced you got this from the anesthesia given during your knee surgery, but we'll never know for sure. Your doctors are also discontinuing your heparin, which is contributing to your NG induced bleeding ulcer.

"This afternoon, your GI bleeding has subsided, somewhat, but when you go into the hiccoughs, the bleeding starts all over again.

"I promise you, Gene, that as long as you hang on, I will hang on. You don't know this, but all our married life, when I have pulled into our driveway and have seen your car in the garage, my heart has literally skipped a beat at the joy of knowing you were home. And when I've pulled into the driveway, and as the garage door opened, if your car was gone, I would be slightly downcast that you weren't home.

"Now, when I come home at night and see your car in the garage, my heart still skips a beat, and then I realize you're not home, and I'm downcast, again.

"You've had so many callers and visitors, it's been absolutely amazing. I don't let them come into your room to see you this way, other than family and close friends, but I visit with them out in the lobby. Every night, when I get home, the answering machine is filled to the end of the tape, and it takes nearly till midnight to answer all the calls. Even the man you ran against for the seat in the House of Representatives telephoned to wish you well.

"Your 4th grade students miss you LOTS, but not as much as I do.

"You've had so much healing today. Big, black bruises are nearly gone, overnight. Weeping sores have dried up and are healing. When the nurse suctioned your lungs, the fluid came out clear. All are good signs. Keep up the good work. I love you."

Gene once had a student who was struck by a car and killed in the crosswalk on her way to school. She happened to be a student for whom he had written a story. It had touched her mother so much, she asked him to speak at the girl's funeral. He was delighted to, and felt it an honor to even be asked.

MARCH 17, 1995

"One of the teachers at your school brought over a packet of handmade get-well cards which your students made for you. As I read them to you, and see their cute little drawings of you, my heart-strings are pulled very tight.

"I stroke your arms and legs and cheeks, as I softly sing to you. I don't know whether or not you can hear me, but the bishop did, when he popped in to visit!

"I find life interesting. I have been so acutely aware of all you have done for me these past twenty-years, which I have taken so much for granted, that if I were blessed to have you live, but had to wait on you hand and foot for the rest of my life, *then* we might be even.

"I taped a large shamrock to your bed today, for good

luck, and I also stuck one on your hospital gown so no one would pinch you for not wearing green. You're losing more platelets today. Your body is eating them up for some reason.

"But, let's be positive: They have changed your stomach pump to an intermittent setting, instead of continual, as your bleeding seems to be subsiding. Your CT scan today showed diminished brain swelling—GREAT news! Keep up the valiant fight, Darling. We all love you so!"

Gene's love for children didn't stop at the teenage level. Each summer, for many years, he and I took high school students on tours to different parts of the world. They loved him and his wry sense of humor. We were always invited to their missionary farewells and wedding receptions. Gene's love was contagious and unprejudiced. He was a wonderful example of accepting others, as Christ would have done.

MARCH 18, 1995

"Hi, Sweetheart. And you are my sweetheart! Forever! I'm reading all your monitors and gizmos. Your respirator has been set at 50%, and you're oxygenating at 95%. Good! Vital signs are all normal. Good! But you perspire so much, it has got to be uncomfortable. Output is good, but you need to get your bowels working again.

"You received flowers today from your school and from our teachers' association (on which Gene served as a member of the Executive board).

"Your condition has been upgraded from very critical to serious. You're showing a little improvement today. Your doctors believe that whatever damage was being done to your brain and central nervous system has now been halted, and that the swelling should continue to recede. We are hopeful."

"No tests of any kind today. They're just going to let you rest and heal. So I will just sit by your side and correct my students' research papers, as it is nearing the end of the term."

During his tenure on the city council, there was one particularly very divisive zoning issue involving physically handicapped children vs. his constituents. Loving children as he did, he voted his conscience on the issue, knowing it would be "political suicide." When he did lose his reelection bid, mostly as a result of that issue, he felt he could still hold his head high and look his Maker in the eye on judgement day.

Following the election, he went to his opponent's house to make peace and to assure his opponent of support, and to offer his assistance whenever needed.

MARCH 19, 1995

"My Dearest Gene, you have some serious problems going on. A normal platelet count is about 140,000. Yours keeps dropping, in spite of the two, eight-pack infusions of platelets you have received. Your count is down to 27,000, which means you bleed very easily and for a very long time. It took three days for the bleeding in your stomach to stop. Everywhere they do a venipuncture, you bleed like a sieve.

"This has caused havoc to your subclavian line. It is constricting circulation to your right arm, which now looks like a balloon. Your arterial line has also caused blocked blood flow. The resulting tissue injury you have sustained from this can become infected and even turn into a "burn." Skin grafts are often necessary when this happens.

"Your poor nose! It looks like raw hamburger where the tubes tear at your nostrils. They would like to do a tracheotomy on you to relieve your poor nose and throat, and to help wean you off the ventilator. But they can't do the surgery as long as you have this bleeding problem due to an exceedingly low platelet count.

"They now need to put a new art line into your other arm, as well as a new subclavian line into your other shoulder, but the same problem exists. Both are surgical procedures, which shouldn't be done, but which need to be done.

"Do you remember I told you ADEM destroys the myelin sheath covering your nerves? The nerves will lay down new myelin, but if scarring occurs as the new myelin is regenerating, you'll never recover fully, and may even become vegetative. Your urine is very dark today. I'm gravely concerned.

"I'm going to church now, down in the hospital chapel. I'll be back in an hour.

"The bishop came in and gave you another blessing this

evening. He turned it over to the Lord, and blessed you that you would be experiencing no pain. You're in grave danger at this time.

"Robert has been very ill with all of this. It is unfortunate he doesn't have the Spirit of the Comforter, with which Jenny and I have been mercifully blessed.

"I must keep positive. Your ventilator has been turned down to 40% oxygen. Your stomach bleeding has stopped. Your vital signs are good. All your organs are functioning.

"It is now 8:00 P.M. and I am exhausted. I will go home to dozens of messages on the answering machine. It has reached the point where I will write down the names and phone numbers and ask someone else to call them back for me."

My weary thoughts have pulled me back to the time when Gene and I lost our full-term baby due to an Rh incompatibility. I had built up antibodies against my own baby which had gone through the placenta and had attacked the fetus I was carrying. These Rh antibodies had eventually destroyed the fetus, and then the dead fetus, in turn, was trying to destroy me. I survived; our baby didn't.

MARCH 20, 1995

"Today I'm so angry, I could spit nails! I was so anxious to get you off from those steroids. Do you remember last Wednesday when they told me they would withdraw them from you, and they would be completely discontinued by yesterday? Well, as of this morning, you're still on four doses a day!

"I questioned your internist and he told me that particular drug was up to your neurologist, who happens to be out of town. I phoned the physician who is supposed to be covering for your neurologist, only to find out he, too, is out of town. Furthermore, the substitute doctor hasn't been in to see you in the five day period your regular neurologist has been out of town. I had a fit! It's as if they have abandoned you.

"There is no way I'm going to wait around for six more days for your regular neurologist to get back into town. You need help NOW!! I'm going to get very testy around here, and you know very well how testy a redhead can be!

"More bad news. They had to change your central subclavian line to the left shoulder, afterall, because the line in the right shoulder clotted off. Now we're all afraid you're going to throw the clot to your lungs, which is nearly always fatal. So now, they're treating you with heparin, again.

"After studying the drug books all night, I am convinced it was the heparin that caused your clot in the first place. I read that a person with severe thrombocytopenia (low platelets) should never be given heparin—that it will actually cause clotting.

"I am extremely anxious."

Early in marriage, there was a family in the ward who, due to unexpected circumstances, were going to go without a Thanksgiving dinner one particular year. After

*ours was prepared, Gene asked the family how they
would feel about taking our meal to the family. The affir-
mative vote was unanimous. The other family was pleas-
antly surprised. Our family felt "warm fuzzies" in spite of
the jam sandwiches we had for dinner that day, and no
one knew about what was done.*

MARCH 21, 1995

"Here I am, bright and early this morning, missing my
morning classes to talk with your physicians again.

"Your internist finally came in and sat down with me. He
looked over two full pages of questions I had written regarding your care, and answered them one by one.

"I asked him about a procedure called plasmapheresis,
which is a treatment I have been reading about. It has the
potential of helping the myelin to not scar as remyelination
takes place. He was familiar with the procedure and promised
to check with the University doctors to see if it would be indi-
cated in your case.

"We talked about your long-term care and about placing
you into an extended care facility, after you come through this.
"He told me he is going to have a hematologist look over
your chart to find out what can be done about your low
platelet count. He is including me in your care planning, and
I am feeling a bit encouraged."

Late afternoon: "After school today, I phoned our insur-

35

ance company to inquire about coverage for an extended care facility. We also verbally agreed that when your benefits have been exhausted, they would then use my coverage, instead. I was happy about this.

"This afternoon, as soon as I entered your room, I knew immediately something was terribly wrong. Your condition has changed dramatically, and everyone is bustling around you.

"Your breathing is labored. Your body is gasping for every breath, like a fish out of water, suffocating, heaves its entire body as it tries to draw oxygen over its gills. I knew immediately that you have thrown the clot to your lungs and that the end is imminent.

"The weather today matches my feelings of impending doom. Heavy, dark clouds envelop the entire valley, and rain is beating against the earth hysterically, as if the hearts of the angels of heaven are weeping with me for a fallen soldier and comrade. My heart hangs as heavily as do the clouds.

"I kissed you tenderly, with all the pent up emotions my aching heart could hold. I told you of my deep and abiding love. And then I relinquished you into God's care.

"You no longer have to hold on for me, Darling. Go and do as you have been called to do. Go with the angels and be free."

This entire scenario had reminded me of when our twenty-three year old son died from brain tumors. Gene was always there for him during the three surgeries, during his recoveries, during visits with the neurosurgeon, and during the related mood swings. Gene was there for him. And, now, who was here for Gene?

MARCH 22, 1995

"I am sitting here beside you, Darling. It's just after midnight. The rain has turned to snow. The cold evening matches the chill in my heart over that which is inevitable. Robert, Jenny, Paul (her husband), and I have been here since 5:30 P.M.

"Your doctor on duty tonight is arrogant and pompous. He and I have already had a run-in. Fortunately, he has only been on your case for two days. Late yesterday afternoon, he wanted to put another arterial line back into your already tremendously damaged right forearm again. He called me at my school to ask for permission, since it was a surgical procedure. I asked him what he specifically hoped to gain that couldn't already be ascertained through other means. I told him of my concern about your low platelet count, as well as the fact that your body had already rejected two art lines, resulting in huge ecchymoses on each arm, and that you had a blood clot in your right SVC. He responded by saying, 'Well, I can see this is a ridiculous conversation,' and hung up on me.

"So, unfortunately, for our family-medical consultation tonight, which we as a family had requested, he is the physician on duty. Although I believe he is overbearing and haughty, he did give us good advice. Together, the family and medical team agreed to continue with your ventilator, so you don't have to struggle so hard to breathe. We agreed to have a continuous morphine IV drip, along with a continuous drip of a sedative to help you relax and ease your pain, if indeed, you are experiencing any."

One oppressive hour blended into the next. At midnight, we determined to discontinue all his lab work, after the lab spent twenty minutes trying to draw some blood which, by then, was futile.

The hospital chaplain had arranged for the four of us to spend the night in empty patient rooms just two doors away from Gene's. The chaplain had correctly surmised that we needed some sleep. Sleep, now that was a rare commodity. Because I had been up all the night before, and was feeling physically exhausted and emotionally drained, I was grateful.

The ICU nurse gently educated us to the fact that sometimes the end could be very disturbing to family members, because the patient oftentimes goes into cardiac arrest, or seizes, or vomits, or any number of other unpleasant things. He also informed us that Gene could be in this final state for up to seventy-two hours, thus encouraging us to get some rest.

At 1:00 A.M., we finally conceded, and asked the nurse to awaken us before the end, that we wanted to be with Gene for his journey to the other side. After reassuring us that he would, we headed to our rooms.

I crashed into a fitful rest, only to be "awakened" at 3:00

A.M. by the nurse, telling me it was time to be with my husband.

The four of us sat around Gene's bed, holding his hands, stroking his arms, kissing him, and telling him of our love. We told him we were grateful for the fact that he had blessed and enriched our lives for twenty-five years.

"My Dear Gene, as you lived with dignity, you died with dignity. There was no heart attack, no seizures, no vomiting— just sweet, peaceful moments which hung in the air. As we watched the monitor, your blood pressure just gradually got lower and lower, until there was no reading at all. At 3:30 A.M., it was over. Your beautiful spirit was freed from its mortal state while we and heaven wept."

CHAPTER TWO

Sixteen days from the time Gene entered the emergency room (eighteen days from his knee surgery), he entered another realm. Gene died from disseminated intravascular coagulation, a complication of the circulatory system. It causes small blood vessels to clot and causes platelets to become depleted. It should have probably been recognized at the first signs of ecchymosis and petechiae so that heparin would not have been given, as it greatly compounds the condition.

The adage "What goes around, comes around," was true with Gene at this time. His ICU nurse on duty the night he entered the hospital was also the same nurse he had the night he passed away.

I found it interesting, and a blessing that both his nurse, as well as the charge nurse on duty that night were males. I asked them if I could remain in the room while they took care of Gene's body for the family to visit. Meanwhile, Robert and Jenny phoned his family and my family to let them know what had just transpired. We intentionally had not called them earlier, as we wanted to be the only ones present with our husband and father at the time.

I was so impressed by the tenderness and respect those

two male nurses gave to my husband as they removed all the hoses, tubing, and machinery. They respectfully bathed his body, keeping it covered the entire time, and then dressed him in a clean hospital gown. They shaved his face and asked if I would like to comb his hair. They then invited our children back into the room to be with their father.

The four of us sat beside him for the last time, awaiting the arrival of family members who had wanted to be there. As we waited, we reminded each other of some of our fondest memories of our husband and dad.

After family members left, the nurses phoned the mortuary. I felt it was another blessing that an autopsy hadn't been required. While we waited for them to arrive, the four of us discussed plans for the funeral.

When the mortician arrived, I asked him if they were going to transport him naked to the mortuary. It was important to me that Gene's dignity was preserved. I was assured that was not done, that what he had on at the moment remained on the body until it was prepared for viewing, and that even then, it was kept draped.

By then it was 6:30 in the morning. We had made an appointment with the mortuary to meet with them at 9:00 to take care of funeral arrangements. Everything went smoothly. We all agreed that the bronze metal casket was suited to Gene's masculinity. Afterwards we went to brunch and reminisced about Gene some more.

Upon arriving at our individual homes afterward, each of us had company for most of the remainder of the day. Jenny and Paul stayed with me for the first two nights, as they didn't want me to be alone. I believe they didn't want to be alone, either.

The funeral went beautifully. Gene's 4th grade class provided some of the music by singing songs Gene had taught them in the school choir. They just sobbed after they performed, which, of course, made everyone else sob. Losing their teacher and hero was very hard on these kids, and the school district had to send out the trauma team to talk with them.

Susan, one of Gene's colleagues, related the following poem, which she had written for the funeral:

My friend came calling today,
His smile would appear;
It spread great cheer
And lightened my burdens some way.

He had such an ease with others,
He cheered up the sad
And made all feel glad,
And was the most wonderful brother.

Concern was his gift to many.
He would search out those to please,
As he'd work through their pain or sorrow—
He'd lighten the day with a tease.

That laughter of his was contagious;
Before long, all would join in.
He never knew why, like a bee to a hive,
He would draw so many others to him.

I've seen him bend down low,
Or pick a child from above—
Filling each with a purpose in life
And telling them stories, with love.

"I want that man for my teacher;
He makes me look and stare.
While waiting for assemblies to start,
He shows us all how he cares."

"Our teacher was very funny;
He changed his mind all the time.
Why, he thought a heart was a bunny,
With a tail, and a little behind."

There never was a friend so dear;
He touched the lives of so many.
All who knew him would give him a cheer
And thank him for teaching them plenty.

If there was a picture to be painted,
Or music that he could sing,
You'd find him there at his easel,
Loving the beauties of Spring.

Yes, our friend came calling each day
With arms outstretched, open wide.
Each child was a son or a daughter
Whom he took to his heart with pride.

Yes, a friend, a husband, a teacher
Was what he did the best.
No one could measure his stature at all;
He'd been put through the hardest of tests.

His memory will live on forever
For all the youth to recall,
That they were blessed to have known him—
Our beloved friend to all.

Now my great friend, I'm letting you go
Off to that fish pond above,
Where you'll be baiting a hook,
While reading a book,
And filling up Heaven with love.

In addition to this poem, I also would like to include excerpts from the talk given by one of Gene's lifelong friends, Barr Woodruff:

"Gene and Patty have been my close friends for many years. We were teenagers who lived in the same neighborhood and ward. This has resulted in a lot of common shared experiences: roadshows, plays, canyon parties, and many hours in his family swimming pool.

"It was great being teenagers in the late fifties. There weren't any drugs, no protesters, no 'R' rated movies. We were able to leave the doors to our houses unlocked. And, believe it or not, we were happy with just three television channels.

"Robert and Jenny, contrary to what your dad

might have told you, we did have indoor plumbing and automobiles.

"When Gene and I were fourteen to fifteen years old, our Sunday School class met on the stage in the cultural hall. There was an old, overstuffed chair on the stage. The rest of the chairs were the hard, folding type. So, every Sunday, at the end of opening exercises, all of the guys in the class raced to have the luxury of lounging in the soft chair during class. Gene spent a lot of Sundays in that chair.

"Sometimes Gene seemed to be a deep thinker, and he would get wrapped up in his own world. There is nothing wrong with this, except when it gets you into trouble. This happened to Gene one particular Sacrament Meeting.

"Gene and I were priests, administering the sacrament. I had just finished saying the blessing on the bread, and as I stood up, Gene was already passing out the trays to the deacons. The problem was that he was passing out the water trays, instead of the bread trays. By the dumbfounded looks on the deacons' faces, Gene was able to rectify the problem.

"Gene was always great at coming up with 'spur of the moment' ideas to try. I'm sure he never told his parents about the one summer evening at the drive-in theater. That particular night, we decided to stay until the last movie ended, which was after 2:00 A.M. As we were driving toward the exit, there happened to be a car full of girls in front of us, so we decided to follow them to their houses. The girls were smarter than we were, because we followed them right into a police station.

"After the police had scrutinized our ID's, they searched the car and found a pair of binoculars in the trunk. Immediately, we were accused of being peeping toms. The sheriff taught Gene and me a great lesson that morning. He told us we had exactly thirteen minutes to get home, or he would call our parents. That was the last thing we wanted to have happen. You have never seen two scared kids drive home so fast, without breaking the law. Of course, we never realized at the time, the sheriff had no intention of calling our parents.

"Because Gene was always the biggest kid in our age group, he ended up playing center on our ward basketball team. He was always under the basket, fighting for those rebounds. He rarely had the opportunity to dribble down the court and make a lay-up. But, one night, he got that opportunity.

"During the game, the opposing team had an inbound play at center court. Gene was able to steal the ball away. He immediately turned around and saw that no one was guarding him, so he dribbled down the court and made a great basket. He was so excited, until he realized he had run the wrong direction and had scored two points for the other team.

"There were five guys in our age group in the ward. We were all active in the church. We all turned nineteen and were looking forward to serving missions. Gene was the first one of us to go on a mission, and we all followed. After our missions, we all graduated from college, and we all got married in the temple. Gene was always dedicated to the Church and to the Lord. He had a great love for the Savior.

"A great philosopher, writer, and runner, George Sheehan, once said, 'Once you have decided that winning isn't everything, you become a winner.' This exemplified Gene. He never patted himself on his own back, or told others how great he was. He was always more concerned about others, their accomplishments and problems.

"Richard L. Evans taught us in one of his sermons, 'We have so much to be grateful for, it almost overwhelms us...thanks for being alive, for the assurance that God lives, that life has meaning and eternal purpose, that life is everlasting, that loved ones live, even after they have left us, that the renewal of association with loved ones is part of our Father's purpose and plan. Thanks to the Savior who taught us of life, and redeemed us from death.'

"We need to remember to pray often and listen to the promptings of the Holy Ghost. If we do, the Lord will bless us. The Savior has said, 'Lo, I am with you always.' Jesus Christ is our older brother who made it possible for each of us to be able to return to our Father's presence. We just have to do our part.

"President Spencer W, Kimball stated, 'No righteous person is taken before his time.' There is comfort in knowing that he is well and is enjoying former friends and family.

"Just as when we were kids, Gene always led the way, he has once again led the way, and is the first one in our group to enter the spirit world. I am sure he will be there to greet each one of us with his unique laugh, happy smile, and crazy sense of humor."

This portion of Gene's story wouldn't be complete if I did not include the other talk given at his funeral, by our dear friend, Hazel Rimmasch:

"Birth and death are not opposites; they are simply two different points on the eternal spectrum. First, we are born to die; and then we die to have eternal life. In the process of birth, we move from eternity into mortality.

"To quote Paul, 'We must crucify the man and come forth in a newness of life in order to go where God and angels dwell.' We must pass beyond this veil of tears to inherit a far greater and grander existence. It is in dying that we are born unto eternal life.

"In mortal death we leave the realms of time and return to the realms of eternity. Life's starkest reality is death. It is the one phase of life we fear most. Not one of us can conquer death in mortality. It is a universal commonality, one which every mortal shares with every other mortal being, in spite of our earthly status or accomplishments.

"Every man and woman is born, and every man and woman must die. We are all born as helpless infants, and we are all equally helpless in the face of death. Joseph Smith taught us that 'the Lord in His wisdom has implanted the fear of death in every person, that they might cling to life, and thus accomplish the designs of their creator.'

"The severance of love and friendship through death is, of all things most painful for those who remain, bringing with it an avalanche of loneliness, heartache and sorrow, bitterness and anguish.

"Patty, Robert, and Jenny, bitter winters will find you walking alone. During the cold and dark seasons of solitude, wrap yourselves in the protective clothing of faith and obedience, and clothe yourselves in the protective armor of God. Be warmed by the precious memories of your lives together with Gene.

"As you are faced with daily challenges, listen carefully. He will always be there for you. He will continue to be your father and husband, gently and patiently teaching you through example. Listen carefully; he will be there for you.

"In a letter Gene wrote several years ago to his father on Father's Day, he wrote, 'In the movie, Superman II, young superman is in his castle in the north country. In the castle he holds a crystal sent with him as an infant from the planet Krypton. This crystal was programmed for the future, when Superman would need help and assistance from his father and mother. Superman was taught what to do in life by the recordings in the crystals. Though his parents were not on earth, their message to their son had a great impact on what Superman would do with his life.

'Our Father in heaven gives us insights into life on this planet Earth. These insights are sent to us through prophets. These messages are sent to us, not in crystals, but in talks, Church publications, lesson manuals, and scriptures. We are also able to communicate with our Heavenly Father through prayer.'

"I have always admired Gene's love for the gospel of Jesus Christ, and how he quietly taught through example. Over the years, as our friendship with Gene and Patty developed, I have truly enjoyed his zest for life. Gene LOVED life. I've never known anyone who could get so excited about preparing and giving a lesson or talk.

"I recall many occasions sitting around the table brainstorming about a political campaign, a school program, taxes, children, animals, diets, or whatever. When differences of opinion were offered, Gene always expressed his appreciation and acceptance of another person's thoughts and values. And we never parted ways without receiving his hug.

"Gene loved to play games. For those of you who didn't have an opportunity to play Scattergories with Gene, you have missed half of your earthly experience. He could come up with a six-point word, while the rest of us struggled to find a one-point word. I laugh at memories of Gene's impish smile as he would concoct a word to win a game of Scrabble with Patty. I think he would really enjoy it when Patty would say, 'Oh, Gene, that's not a word,' and challenge him to look it up in the dictionary. After making a half-hearted attempt to locate the word, he would slap the dictionary down on the table and declare, 'Well, it was there last week.'

"Gene loved to go fishing. He loved taking his

children fishing and teaching them about God's creations and the outdoors. I remember the day when Jenny caught her first fish at three years old. He was more excited than she was.

"Gene was an avid fisherman. More importantly, he was a fisher of men, always guiding and directing his family in righteousness, always walking straightway to serve his Father in Heaven.

"Gene loved so many aspects of life, but let me share for a moment what Gene loved more than life. Gene loved Patty during her waking hours. Gene loved Patty while she slept. Gene loved Patty when she laughed and when she cried. Gene loved Patty when she was doing for him and for others. Gene loved his very best friend, his wife, his lover, his everything.

"Patty had to be careful what she said, because if Gene felt she wanted something, he would provide it. It could be late at night, watching an ad on TV, and if Patty stated, 'Doesn't that hot fudge sundae look yummy?' Upon the very utterance of her words, Gene had his pants and coat on and was gone to get the hot fudge sundae.

"Gene and Patty were inseparable. They did everything together, and up until a couple of days ago, you seldom saw one without the other. Aristotle is known for a quote, which sums up Gene and Patty's relationship together. He said, 'Friendship is one soul in two bodies.'

"Gene found one of his favorite sayings while shopping in a boutique one day with Patty, and he bought it to hang on their kitchen wall. He called us with laughter and joy in his voice, informing us he had found the perfect plaque that day. It states, 'My wife and I have an understanding: I don't try to run her life, and I don't try to run mine.'

"So what did Gene do with Patty besides love her and care for her, you ask? He mopped and vacumed, cooked meals and bottled fruit. He groomed the yard, shoveled the walks, maintained the cars, paid the bills, washed the clothes, the dishes, and the windows, made the bed, prepared their taxes, and...and...and...he loved Patty.

"Patty received a FAX from Warsaw, Poland this week. It said, in part, 'I would like to share a few thoughts as to why I consider Gene such a good friend and example. I will never forget the love and respect with which he always treated his family. I was always amazed at how much love he showed his dear wife. I truly feel that he loved Patty more than anything on this earth. I don't just say that; I truly mean it. In my entire life, I never once recall hearing an angry tone in Gene's voice while being around Patty. His example is one I will never forget.'

"Gene's son, Robert, handed me a letter this morning that he had written to his father. I asked him if I could quote from it during the funeral. What he had to say truly personifies Gene's Christ-like qualities. He wrote, 'You were the consummate peacemaker, Dad. Everyone's needs came before your own. You always did whatever it took to make others feel better—no easy task. I know your whole life you dreamed and worked to be financially successful, so you could do all the things you wanted to for others, like sending kids on missions, feeding the hungry, helping the needy. This week I realized that, although you never got your financial 'break,' you accomplished your dream on a daily basis: one person, one deed, one gift at a time.'

"If we could hear Gene's voice right now, I believe these would be the words he would share with us: 'Friends are a choice breed of people. There are all kinds in the world; some I've had for years; some I have just met. And, some I have yet to meet. God has been very kind to me because He has given me a variety of lovely people in my life. I hope I have given one small portion of myself to each of you who, in your own special ways, have given so much of yourselves to me. I hope that I will always have a place within your hearts, because each of you have had a very special place in mine.

"'I am grateful to my heavenly Father for letting me share in each of your lives. He has been most kind to me. Each of you, in your own ways, have added just the right ingredients in my life: kindness, understanding, patience, love, laughter, the sharing of confidences, and just the right words which let me know I was important to you. I love you all.

> "*Do not stand by my grave and weep.*
> *I am not there. I do not sleep.*
> *I am a thousand winds that blow.*
> *I am a diamond glint on snow.*
> *I am the sunlight on ripened grain.*
> *I am the gentle Autumn rain.*

"'When you awake in the morning hush,
I am the swift, uplifting rush
Of quiet birds in circling flight.
I am the soft starshine at night.
Do not stand by my grave and cry.
I am not there. I did not die.'"

Part Two

SURVIVAL

CHAPTER THREE

If anyone were to have asked how I was doing on Easter Day, nearly four weeks after Gene's death, I was still numb, which was good, I suppose. In a way, that numbness must be nature's general anesthesia to help block the pain of a loved one's death. Gene was so vital, so alive. It was still hard to believe that he was really gone and was not coming back.

My emotions were so labile, up and down, and up and down. I cried so much my eyelids became swollen, and my eyeballs, too, were so swollen at times that my vision became distorted. My irritated throat and nasal passages felt like a cold was coming on but, of course, one never developed. It was just that they were swollen, as well.

Neighbors were super! Even the neighborhood children brought me plates of cookies and hand-printed cards. Meals were brought in. I was phoned, visited, and taken out. Nevertheless, the loneliness was still there to taunt me when the visiting was over. Every song on the radio took on an entirely new meaning. Ofttimes a thought would strike me, and the memory would freshen the tears.

One of my neighbors was a physician who taught classes at the University School of Medicine. He researched ADEM and disseminated intravascular coagulation (DIC) for me and was able to bring me quite a bit of literature. After pouring over this information, I was convinced that this was simply Gene's time to die. There was no other explanation for it. But, it did leave me with many unanswered questions.

I met with my stake patriarch regarding Gene's blessing which stated two different times that his days would be long upon the earth. He told me that President Spencer W. Kimball has said there is no such thing as an untimely death if a man is righteous, and that everything is numbered and planned for by the Lord—a time to live and a time to die. When I asked for a reference, he directed me to the Ensign, "A Star of the First Magnitude," Dec. 1985, pg. 33.

Soon, I had to call upon a neighbor for help, which officially placed me in the "helpless widow" category. A terrible windstorm had blown out the pilot light to my furnace. When I awakened to April snow the following morning, the furnace wouldn't function.

Fixing it was something Gene could have easily handled, and I missed him again. I called a repair service and was willing to pay them to check it out for me. All the places I called were swamped, and I was cold, so I had to resort to calling upon a neighbor, which didn't please me. I had always been fairly independent (as long as Gene was around), and I wasn't too keen on the idea of being a helpless widow. I just hated asking anyone for help!

Furthermore, I couldn't quite cope with the stigma of my status in the Church being changed from "normal" to "special interest." Whoever coined that phrase was definitely not single. If that weren't bad enough, I became further stigmatized by not being a "young" special interest! I still thought of myself as a "couple." A couple didn't have any social stigmas associated with it, and that was still what I was, at least in my mind. But, on Church records, I was now stigmatized as a "special interest," which meant that I was probably "supposed" to sit on the back row of the chapel with the other single sisters in the ward. It wasn't that I didn't love them dearly, but I wanted to sit where Gene and I had always sat.

Sundays were especially hard. Those were together days for Gene and me. Because we didn't watch television on Sundays, we spent the day visiting someone, reading the Ensign or studying scriptures together, going to church together, or playing board games or dominoes, or, in the summer, playing badminton or croquet.

I just rattled around on Sundays, like a lost puppy, weeping and generally feeling sorry for myself. I decided to invite people over to dinner on Sundays to help fill in the blank spaces with others whom I loved. That helped.

Nights were also lonely. During the day, when the sun ruled the sky, the daily hub-bub kept me occupied. But, at night, when the sun would set and the lights would come on, I found my spirits sinking with the setting sun. That was when I was left alone, with only the company of my thoughts and a box of tissues. And, my king-sized bed was so big and so empty.

The bishop visited about a week following the funeral to see how I was doing. The question was raised, would I ever marry again? At that time, my answer was "probably not." My husband was perfection personified. Who else in the world could be as good as he was? And, why should I settle for anything less, just to be "married?" I didn't mind being alone, compared to the alternative—dating! Or being married to a lesser man.

My dog kept me company. I loved my ward. I loved my neighbors. I loved my home, which Gene had bought for me. We had four years of complete happiness in our new home. It was filled with beautiful memories, which I shall always treasure. To have moved at that time was out of the question. It was my haven and my sanctuary. To have moved would have been to close Gene out of my life, and I wasn't ready to do that.

I took the time to compile a scrapbook of the last three weeks of Gene's life. I gleaned pleasure working on it. It became a loving memory of the missing half of my life. Each page was filled with love. And, I finally got one hundred and forty-five thank you cards written and mailed.

Another problem I had was in going to work. I just hated driving out to 4800 West to go to my school. It had suddenly become very far away, and I just wanted to be near the haven of my home. That first week following Gene's death, I had to force myself to go to work. With each succeeding block I would drive, I would feel as if I were going to drive off the edge of the earth. Each day became worse.

Knowing I still had ten weeks left in the school year, I didn't know how I was going to handle this particular stress, so I took my problem to the Lord. The following morning, as I was turning onto 4800 West, it dawned on me that those feelings of dread hadn't consumed me. The next day, as I was driving home, I realized that those dreadful feelings hadn't occupied my mind at all. Driving to work was okay after that.

Over the weeks I took care of all the tedious things, such as changing the utilities into my name, meeting with benefits personnel at the school district, having Gene's state retirement transferred over, going to the Social Security office, changing bank accounts and signature cards, making insurance claims, and meeting with my attorney to update our trust.

I also had to meet with an insurance claims investigator, because Gene's insurance policy had not been in effect for the required two years. I met with my insurance agent and investment agent, figured out what to do with Gene's car, and had the auto insurance changed. I paid off the mortuary, had our income taxes prepared, and made a new portfolio for my children, in the event of my demise. Interestingly, it took about a year for all the paperwork to be finalized.

I wasn't real anxious to do anything in particular with Gene's car right away, so I just continued to make payments on it until I did decide what to do. My car was a good car, which fit my short frame. Gene's car was a luxury car, but was too large for me. I had to sit on a pillow in order to drive it. The question was, which car would I keep and which one would I sell? After a couple of months, I decided to sell both of them and get myself a luxury car in my size.

Gene and I had been planning to take a group of high school students on a trip to the British Isles that summer, as we had done for the previous five years, but to different locales. I reluctantly decided to keep my role as the teacher-leader and go on the trip with the students. I knew it would be hard to attend to those duties without my companion, but the other couple we had traveled with would be there to support me. I also knew it would have been hard to stay at home, knowing Gene would have wanted me to go on the trip. That helped me to make up my mind to go.

I decided to also take my children and son-in-law on a short vacation that summer. We had just been torn apart, and I felt the family needed to bond, and talk, and reestablish our love for each other. I felt Gene would have wanted me to use some of the money he left me for that purpose.

Regardless of the number of times I had wished for death to consume me, as it had done my husband, through study and prayer, I came to realize there was a purpose for me to continue living. I had no idea what it was, but I believed God had a plan for me. I knew that if I were submissive to His will, that plan would be fulfilled. That was when I learned to walk by faith.

I learned that life is fragile and can be obliterated in a single act, or it can be eliminated slowly over a longer period of pain and suffering. I realized that one's testimony is also fragile and can be shattered into oblivion by a million outside forces piercing its delicate nature. It, too, can be obliterated in a single act, or be eliminated slowly over a longer period of pain and suffering. This is why our testimonies must be constantly nurtured. When we question God, or demand explanations for which there are no mortal answers, we are only setting ourselves up for sorrow.

Part Three

TRANSITION

CHAPTER FOUR

At the end of the four month mark, Robert came to see me to inform me I was depressed and that I needed counseling. I asked him what made him think that I was depressed. Was I sleeping too much, or not enough? Was I overeating, or not eating at all? Was I letting my house and yard go to ruin? Was I not taking care of my health, or grooming, or hygiene? Was I being irresponsible to my commitments? Was I not getting out? Was I crying all the time? In answering "no" to all these questions, he admitted that he was probably projecting his own depression onto me, and that maybe he was the one who needed counseling.

I explained to him that I have a counselor who is free of charge anytime I need to visit with him, and that I don't even have to make an appointment, or leave my house, or find a parking lot to do so. I have only to take the avenue of prayer to visit with my counselor—God.

Although Robert has chosen to no longer be associated with the Church, he knows enough about it to realize it is something I absorbingly believe in. I reminded Robert that I had been blessed with the Spirit of the Comforter, which he had forfeited. In 2 Nephi 32:5, we have been told that if we receive the Holy Ghost, it will tell us all things that we should do. What a great privilege it is to have the companionship of a member of the Godhead!

I also had the blessing of the veil being quite thin at times, and Gene had been able to communicate with me to ease my grief and restore comfort to my life.

One evening, two weeks following his death, I was feeling extremely lonely and was in great need of comfort. As I was lying in bed, during that sweet time when the mind reviews the day's events and starts to yield to slumber, Gene came into my mind. He said, "I am here for you." I explained to him how I hated going to bed alone at night. He told me guardian angels would watch over me every night, so I would never need to fear. (To this day, I have never been afraid.)

I told him of my concerns about going on the trip with the high school students in the summer. He told me all would go well on the trip (and it did). He promised that my health would be fine on the trip (and it was), but that he couldn't promise that I wouldn't get tired (and I did).

Jennifer and Paul were having some conflict over a certain matter, which I wanted to have resolved. I asked Gene, in my mind, what I could say or do to help them find a solution without hurting feelings. He told me the opportunity would arise where it would be given to me what to say, when the time came. (This did transpire just as Gene promised, and the conflict was settled.)

I told Gene I didn't want to go to sleep, because I was enjoying being with him so much. I knew that when sleep overcame me, Gene would be gone. He responded by telling me, "I will always be here for you, if you believe." This was such a tender experience, I shall always treasure it.

Another sweet experience was on Mother's Day. My kind sister didn't want me to be alone on this day, so she invited me to her home for a family get-together.

As I got into my car and pulled out of the driveway, I said aloud, "Come on Gene, I'll take you for a ride in my new car." He did come along, and was there for the entire drive to my sister's house, which was only ten minutes away. We communicated through our thoughts. I asked him questions, and he would answer them. There were two reasons my mind wasn't playing tricks on me. The first reason was that I was receiving answers to questions to which I previously had not known the answers. The second reason was the literal presence I felt with my husband at the time.

Nearing my sister's house, I didn't want to stop the car. I knew as soon as I stopped the engine and got out, that sweet experience would be gone. I was weeping because I wanted to drive into oblivion with the company of my husband, but I knew I could not.

One day, shortly after Gene's funeral, I was driving to school, and audibly cried out in anguish, "Oh, Gene, why did you have to die at such a terrible time of year? If you had waited until the end of summer, we could have celebrated our 25th wedding anniversary. You could have gone on the trip with me this summer, as we had planned. You could have taken care of our IRS audit. You would have prepared our annual tax return. Why did you have to die when you did?"

Gene's gentle thoughts came into my mind again. He told me the audit would be taken care of—anyway. Our income taxes would be figured out—anyway. I'd be going on the trip—anyway. He reminded me of the hundreds of times I had told people how I was so thankful there were only ten weeks left in the school year, and how I had lamented that if Gene had died at the beginning of the school year, I wouldn't have known how I could have handled it, because those final ten weeks were agony for me. Gene told me that if he had died at the beginning of the school year, I would have had a terrible time. He was right! As it was, I had the summer to recover, somewhat. He reminded me that there really was no "good" time for a loved one to die. He told me he was sorry for missing our anniversary, but that these things are only mortal experiences—anyway. By then I was parking the car, and the conversation, unfortunately, terminated.

The bishop gave me a new calling, that of education counselor in the Relief Society. I was set apart on May 21st. Some very specific statements were told me during the setting apart, which were answers to questions I had had on my mind. He told me during the blessing that the Lord wanted me in that calling at that time because my talents and my experiences would be of benefit to others in the ward. He assured me that my sins were forgiven me. Then he paused for an uncomfortably long time, and then started to weep.

After he regained control, he blessed me by informing me that Gene was there to witness the setting apart, and that he was proud of me. He continued, "Gene wants you to know that he'll be there for you whenever you need his help." I already knew this because of the previous experiences I had enjoyed.

By then, the bishop was weeping; I was weeping; and, my Relief Society president was weeping. After I was set apart for my new calling, instead of the usual handshake, the bishop gave me a big old bear hug, as did everyone in the room. It was great!

A new gospel doctrine teacher was finally called to take Gene's place—three months following his funeral. I felt this was a decent length of time. For some petty reason, I would have been hurt if the position had been filled right away. The day the new teacher was sustained in Sacrament Meeting, the bishop caught me in the hall and said, "You noticed I didn't release Gene from his calling. That's because I wanted him to teach Gospel Doctrine right into eternity." I smiled and thanked him for his sensitivity.

Our dear friend, Hazel, had to have their fourteen-year old dog put to sleep due to some serious health problems. It broke her heart. As she was driving home from the veterinarian's office, she prayed that God would allow her to know that Toby (her dog) understood, and that he would be taken care of and not be abandoned. At that moment, she distinctly heard Gene's voice calling, "Here, Toby. Come here, boy." His voice was so clear she turned to the back seat to see if Gene were there. This was so comforting to her, and she knew her prayer of love for her dog had been answered.

This brings to mind another experience Jennifer and Paul had around that same time. They had lost their kitten, Makita, to the hands of an unpleasant neighbor. They had been grieving over their poor cat, not knowing if it were dead or alive, but suspecting the former. One night, Jennifer dreamed she was in her back yard playing with her dogs. Suddenly, Makita came out from behind a large pine tree and romped over to her. As Jennifer was playing with Makita, Gene came out from behind the same tree and picked Makita up in his arms and told Jenny, "Don't worry about 'Keeters,' I'll take good care of her."

When Jennifer related her dream to her husband the following morning, he explained to her that he had dreamed the very same dream, only he had interpreted the dream as taking place in the mountains, not in the back yard, because of the large pine tree.

There is life after death, for both our loved ones and our pets. I have to believe that. Why else would those experiences have happened? The lives we love are being cared for on the other side. We just have to stop being so impatient to get there, and continue taking care of our mortal and spiritual estate while we still have the chance.

All these experiences through the veil had transpired during the four months since Gene's death. They comforted my grieving soul and strengthened my faith.

Those four months were busy in mortal ways, as well. I decided to get closet organizers for Gene's and my closets. It was something we had talked about doing prior to his death. This decision forced me to go through Gene's clothes. I was happy to be able to find people who could use them and who could fit into his large sizes.

Once I had gone through his clothes, I decided I may as well go through his dresser drawers, as well. Having done that, I decided to attack his night stand and his bathroom drawers. Then I decided it was time to clean out my own closet and drawers.

My mind wouldn't settle for only part of my house being extraordinarily cleaned, so then I delved into the kitchen cupboards, shelves, and pantry. When the kitchen shined, I tore into the living room and other closets. Within a couple of weeks, the entire main level of my house was thoroughly cleaned. Well, it wouldn't do to have only one level of my house clean, so I tackled the basement next, saving the upstairs until last. I was dreading the upstairs. It was where Gene's office was located, and I knew it would be hard to go through his things there.

The inevitable time came when I had to clean the upstairs. It took a couple of days to clean out my office. Gene's was the last room in the house to clean. It was hard going through all of his business things. There were "treasures" of when he served on the city council. There were all his tax clients' files to be taken care of. There were "treasures" from Church, and his personal "treasures" to be catalogued, saved, and filed. I came across many papers he had written, of which I hadn't even been aware, dealing with his testimony of the gospel.

Some of his effects stated, "Write down my basic understanding of the gospel of Jesus Christ," but he hadn't gotten around to doing that, unless it was put onto a computer disk. I had yet to go through his hundreds of disks.

On a slip of scratch paper he had scribbled, "When we meet the Savior and receive our just reward, no person will be able to place blame on another. When we are allowed to recall our every thought, our every act, our every choice in this life, we will say it is just. We have many opportunities to exercise change from where we are to where Christ is. Christ set the example of supreme love. He invites us to express this love in our lives because we choose to, not because we are compelled to."

On another slip of paper, I saw his notes entitled, "What

I Gained From Conference." He wrote: "I gained a testimony of our new prophet. I have a knowledge that my Father in Heaven loves me—loves us all. I learned that I must avoid anything that would prevent my spirit from listening to and understanding personal revelation when I need it. I must do the simple things I am asked to do, and not look for the grandiose things to receive approval from men. Good, spiritual music has a positive power and influence on my soul."

In going through his desk, I came upon another scrap of paper which sent chills down my spine. On that little slip of paper, in his top desk drawer, was written, "Make a list of personal items in my school room, to be on file in case of death, to authorize their removal." I sat paralyzed, thoughts orbiting my mind. Did Gene know he was going to die?

My mind went spinning back to last fall when Gene told me he dreamed he was going to die and that he'd better clean out his school closet and organize his classroom things. I had fluffed it off. He had dreamed on other occasions of certain people dying, but those events had never transpired. So, why should his dream mean anything then?

A few months later, he told me he'd had the same dream, and again, a third time, a few weeks later. One would think I would have caught on and questioned Gene, in depth, about his dreams. Obviously, I was off in Nirvana, and I regretted the lack of follow through on my part.

But the stories! Oh, the stories I found—scores and scores of them. Gene was a talented writer. He always took a notepad with him wherever he went, because the slightest incident would spark a flood of ideas in his creative mind. How he would get frustrated at not being able to write them down as fast as the ideas would come to him.

Gene wrote stories for neighborhood children. he wrote stories about his students. He wrote stories for individuals and for no one in particular. I stored all his stories in a huge box. My deepest desire is to go through his stories and edit and publish them. Who knows how many more I'll find on his computer disks. If I didn't have to work, that is how I'd spend my days for the next several years.

I came upon a parable Gene had written for our daughter when she was about twelve:

"Once there was a fish who said he would never be caught. A clever fisherman said, 'We'll see.' Daily, the clever fisherman put a worm into the stream by the fish, until the day came when he put the worm on a hook. The unsuspecting fish was used to eating worms, and swallowed the worm on the hook. The fisherman tugged hard on the line to set the hook, and then the fish was caught. Satan tempts us the same way. We only think we get away with doing the little things Satan wants us to do. But, sooner or later, we'll be caught with his hook. We need to be mindful to follow Jesus. That is the only way we'll ever remain free."

I came across so many things in Gene's office—hundreds and hundreds of papers on which he had written ideas which he had wanted to, one day, complete. But, he never had the time to see his ideas to fruition, because the ideas would come to him faster than he had hours in the day to complete. He was very definitely held back by our mortal time frame. His creative mind worked faster than any mortal body could keep up with.

Gene was a 4th grade teacher whom his students adored. He developed brilliant and innovative ways in which to teach certain concepts. He had a Master's Degree in education. He served two terms on the Executive Board of our teachers' association, and was seeking a third term at the time of his death. He attended national conferences. He served on the city council. He ran for other political offices because he felt a tremendous love for his country and felt he had a duty to help preserve our freedoms and our heritage. He loved to dabble in oil painting and water colors and would take his easel out on our deck to paint in the out-of-doors. He loved music and could happily listen to everything from opera to country western. He had a nice voice, and we would sometimes sing duets in church. He sang in the ward choir. He prepared income taxes for people. He was an optician and made contact lenses, a trade he had learned before becoming a teacher. He had served a mission to Mexico and spoke Spanish fluently.

As I went through Gene's office, it dawned on me, very clearly, that his many talents were going to be utilized much better in the hereafter, where he wouldn't be bound by the time constraints and limitations of mortality.

When his office was finally cleaned and organized, I knew Gene was pleased. It took many, many days to complete, but I treasured each of them.

I realized that the only "room" in the house not cleaned now was the garage. I organized Gene's workbench and tool chests. I sold his bicycle. Each shelf became orderly and neat. Finally, my house and my life seemed to be in order.

In all of the cleaning I accomplished, I found pounds and pounds of hard, wrapped candies. They were in virtually all of his suit jackets. Candy was in his coat pockets. I found candy in his dresser drawers, his night stand drawers, and in his desks at school and at home. Candy was also on top of his desk at home, in a mug for his tax clients to draw from. It was in his closets and in the pockets of many of his trousers. He loved to give it away.

He would gave candy to a crying child in church. He tossed candy to his students as they called out correct answers to questions. He gave it to his "starving" wife and children when our tummies were growling in church or at the movies. He kept candies in the glove box of his car. He was known as the "candy man."

Gene's elementary school invited me to a special program they held in his honor. The entire fourth grade class sang songs he had taught them in his choir. With money which had been donated to Gene's school, in his behalf, they had purchased a huge flowering peach tree and were going to plant it just outside Gene's classroom window. I thought that was a fitting reminder of his devotion to his teaching profession and to his students, as well as the devotion his students held for him.

During our ward conference a few weeks following Gene's funeral, a member of our stake presidency and a member of our bishopric came to visit me. I reiterated my frustration over Gene's patriarchal blessing which stated his days would be long upon the earth.

The counselor in the stake presidency told me something which I hold dear. He said, "Patty, with all that Gene accomplished, he did live long upon the earth. He accomplished more than most people do in longer lifetimes. He lived long enough to see you through your schooling. He lived long enough to see you get a stable job. He lived long enough to move you into this beautiful home and wonderful ward. He lived long enough to see his family raised. He lived long enough to see his son, Todd, through his debilitating illness and subsequent death. He lived long enough to see his youngest daughter married. He lived long enough to do a lot of traveling with you. He lived nearly a quarter of a century with you. He lived long enough to assure you of his love. So, you see, Patty, Gene did live long upon the earth—long enough."

Two months later, my nephew and his wife took me out to dinner. His comment on the subject was this: "Maybe the time for Gene's days to be 'long upon the earth' will be during the Millennium, when the veil will be so thin that the Saints of Heaven will be able to work closely with the Saints on Earth to bring to pass the genealogy and temple work which will need to be done. Maybe he'll have a thousand years in which to 'be upon the earth.'" I found comfort in these thoughts, also.

Was life any easier four months following his death? In some ways, yes; in other ways, no. I had invited the single sisters in the ward over to my home for Sunday dinners. Those times were most delightful experiences. Summer was drawing to a close, and I had to get into the mindset of school starting again in the next three weeks. My health had been good. I had been adjusting to my new Church calling and was enjoying it very much.

There was still an unsettling feeling gnawing at me. I was still feeling incomplete—one body and soul, when there should have been two! Most of the couples we had done things with stopped asking me out. That hurt! It was definitely a "couples-only" society. I had a long way to go in adapting to my recently acquired single status. I found I had to keep myself busy, or else I would have too much time to think. And every time I would think, I would cry.

Nights became easier. Nevertheless, I can't explain the countless times I would look at Gene's side of the bed during the night, only to focus on an empty pillow. There were numerous times I had turned over during the night, hoping to not disturb Gene, only to remember he wasn't there.

Oftentimes during the nights, I felt the shifting of weight on the mattress, thinking it was Gene, stirring, but would realize it was only my dog, Tootsie.

One balmy summer morning, as the breeze floated through the open window above our bed, I dearly missed Gene's beautiful face, his smile, his strong body and gentle touch. I missed the lazy summer morning neck rubs or back rubs. I missed holding his hand. I missed Gene!

At the five month point, summer was quickly coming to a close, and I thought life would be easier. But it was as if my grieving process had begun all over again. As I ironed clothes, I found there was too much time to think, and when I had time to think, the tears would begin anew. In balancing the checkbook each month, I would see Gene's handwriting in the check register, and the tears would flow again. Hymns sung in church took on entirely different meanings, for example, "God Be With You Till We Meet Again" made the tears flow effortlessly.

Living alone, so suddenly, had been a difficult adjustment. When things around the house would break down and need repair—things I had always been able to depend upon Gene to readily fix—I would struggle with unfamiliar tools and little mechanical sense to accomplish the things he was so adeptly able to do. At times, when I had to submit to seeking help from a neighbor, tears of frustration would start all over again. At other times, when I was more in tune with the Spirit of the Comforter, I would literally hear promptings as to how to go about solving a particular household problem.

Little things, like reaching high and awkward places, as when changing outdoor lightbulbs, for example, became monumental tasks. Thoughts of decorating my house for various holidays, which was something Gene and I loved to do together on a monthly basis, were depressing.

I found I needed to keep every minute filled, because any spare time brought memories of Gene, and then I was just one big tear duct.

My logical mind would tell me that Gene was better off in immortality, and that those moments of grief and anger which I had experienced were merely the results of selfishness on my part. I wanted Gene here to fill my life, to give me a purpose for living, to love me, to hold me, to rub away the tension in my neck and shoulders, to be my sounding board, to play games with, to travel with, to visit with, to be company for me in an empty, lonely house, and to take care of me— me—me. I realized that grief was a purely selfish attitude, but that knowledge didn't make the loss any easier to handle.

I loved Gene dearly. I was so thankful for the legacy of love, strength, integrity, and example he left behind for all who knew him.

CHAPTER FIVE

As the days of summer drew to a close, I had become acutely aware of all the summertime things Gene and I had done together, and I really missed my golfing partner and my traveling companion. During the course of that summer, I went on one walk, I rode my bike one time, I golfed one time, and I felt starkly alone.

At least twice a year, often more, Gene and I had given great parties. We have always had a beautiful yard and have very much enjoyed entertaining. There were no yard parties that year. I felt as if our beautiful yard had been wasted. There had been no badminton games, no croquet games, no barbecues, no picnics. There had been only yard work to do, and with no one to help me with it. It renewed my appreciation of him even more. And, there was no one to repair broken sprinkler heads.

The fruit from our trees was given away that summer. There was no longer a need to preserve or dehydrate it, since there was only me, now. Gene and I had always picked the fruit together and had either canned it or dehydrated it together. Our two-man effort cut the work dramatically and made hard work light. It had been difficult to pick the fruit myself that summer, especially in the uppermost branches. I had to ask someone, again, to bail me out. I hated doing that!

Elder Russel M. Nelson wrote "Mourning is one of the purest expressions of deep love" (*The Gateway We Call Death,* p.22). And in the Doctrine and Covenants 42:45, we are instructed, "Thou shalt live together in love insomuch that thou shalt weep for them that die."

I had missed Gene so much, especially the entire last week of summer, just before having to return to school. I found myself sniveling night and day, hardly letting up for anything. I think it must have been a combination of things which made me miss him so much. Simply going back to face another year of school was reason enough, but there were other reasons, as well.

That week my sadness deepened to the point where I was nonfunctional much of the time. I knew I had to pull myself together before the school year started the following week, but I just didn't know how I was going to go about it.

Teaching had been so much a part of our lives together. Gene and I would look forward to returning back to school each fall. We'd have holidays off at the same time. We'd have our summers off at the same time. During the summertime, we were twenty-four hour a day roommates who adored being with each other.

We both were actively involved with our teachers' association—Gene was on the Executive Board for several years, and I was an Association Representative from my school for those same years. Many activities in the association drew us together in work.

At the end of each summer, when we'd have to return to school the week preceding the students, Gene and I would meet somewhere for lunch. This seemed to make that transition week, before the onslaught of students, more bearable. Gene would always take a day to help me set up my classroom, putting up bulletin boards and posting pictures high on the walls where I had wanted them, but couldn't reach.

That coming year, there would be no help. There would be no meeting for lunch. There would be no collaboration in preparing lesson plans. There would be no mutual work within the association. There would be no one with whom to share amusing anecdotes or to be a sounding board for problems.

In short, school up to that time had been fun and enjoyable. I had been enthusiastic in my teaching. I had looked forward to the challenges each day would bring. Gene had asked me on one occasion what I would do if I won a lottery. "I'd continue to teach, of course," I had replied.

Not anymore. I'd have quit teaching in a minute if I'd had the opportunity. I knew I would be facing a major attitude problem that school year. Instead of working for enjoyment, I'd be working out of necessity. Instead of having the option of not having to teach, I knew I would now have to teach the rest of my life. Somehow, that changed things.

I remembered that Gene had told me on two different occasions since his passing, that if I ever needed him, he would be there for me. Well, I needed him in a very real way. I prayed and asked heavenly Father if Gene could meet me in our local temple at a specific time.

I went through a temple session and waited at the specified time and felt no inspiration. After thirty minutes, I finally closed my eyes. It was then that distinct thoughts entered my mind.

I had been taking some pretty strong ulcer medication

which had been having some adverse effects. I asked if I should continue with it or not. I was told that, unfortunately, I would be subject to the laws of mortality, but to continue taking the medication for the remaining five days.

I wondered if my daughter and son-in-law would ever have children in this life and was told there were spirit children waiting to come to them, but that it would be up to them to take care of whatever physical problems they may have in order to get them here.

I wondered if I should run for our city council. I knew there were only two other candidates, and I knew I could beat both of them in an election. I could literally envision myself sitting on the council dias each week. But I was torn as to whether or not it would have been the right thing for me to do. The thoughts came into my mind that it was not the right thing for me to do *because* I would be elected, and the Lord had other things He wanted me to do, which I would not have been able to do if I had a four year commitment to the city.

I told Gene, in my mind that my emotions had been so labile—that one continuous tear couldn't be distinguished from the next, and there was no way I would be able to start school in my present frame of mind. I asked Gene to give me a blessing.

The words to his blessing entered my mind. "I bless you that you will be fine. You're strong and no less a survivor than anyone else who has gone through the death of a spouse. I miss you as much as you do me, but the time when we are together again will be short, I promise you. Earth life is so short in the eternal realm.

"Your faith is stronger than you give yourself credit for. Don't put yourself down. You have many beautiful qualities.

Many women who may be more physically alluring, lack many of the beautiful qualities you have.

"Smile. Have a happy countenance, and the attitude of happiness will follow. I love you and always will. Keep being faithful, and we will be together again. I love you dearly.

"I have to go now—

"I have to go now—

"I have to go now."

After returning home, I read in *Teachings of the Prophet, Joseph Smith,* "Departed spirits are not far from us, and know and understand our thoughts, feelings, and emotions, and are often pained therewith" (320).

I felt so much better. By the following day I had enough energy and peace of mind to go to my school and begin to prepare for my students. I must admit, however, that my attitude about *having* to work persisted throughout the entire year.

One of the teachers at my school, who had known us since we were first married, caught me in the copy room during that hectic first week of school. He remarked, "You know, Gene didn't leave you many options."

"What do you mean?" I asked.

"Well, it's not like Gene was a bum, so that if you remarried, anyone would be a step up. In fact, Gene was the kind of guy who was practically perfect in every way. There aren't too many men like him. So that leaves you in the quandary: Do I want to marry down, just to be remarried? Or, do I want to stay single the rest of my life because no one can match up to Gene?"

He had verbalized what had been on my mind. How insightful. I just smiled and told him he was right on target.

At just about the same time teachers had to return to school in August, it was also the time of our annual County Fair. Gene and I had always gone to the County Fair because the fairgrounds had been so close to where we had lived for 18 years, and it was free. That year was the first year I didn't attend. I hadn't wanted to go alone, nor had I particularly felt in a festive mood.

Two weeks into the school year, I came down with a rousing bout of the twenty-four hour flu. As I was holding my head over the commode, I was reminded again of my dear husband.

Whenever I had been ill, he had been there for me—to hold my hand, offer me a cool wash-cloth, sit with me, comfort me, and to dote over me. That time, he wasn't there, and I felt truly abandoned. There was no one to help me off the bathroom floor, tuck me into bed, see if I was comfortable, answer the phone, or to wait on me. Nor was he there to give me a blessing. I had to call upon someone other than my husband for the first time in twenty-five years, which was hard to do.

I couldn't help but wonder what would happen if I were to ever need surgery. In the past, Gene would have been there to transport me to and from the hospital, sit with me night and day, and wait on me at home after I had been released. Just knowing he would be there would be such a tremendous source of comfort and strength to me that I would actually feel myself heal. Dark thoughts troubled my mind over this.

Then I remembered one particular day that Gene performed a supreme act of love and sacrifice for me. A few years ago, I had been ill during the night and wasn't any better by morning. Gene called the substitute office for me, only to be told there were no substitutes available. The woman on the phone did mention, on the sly, that if I had needed an elementary substitute, there were still some available, but that all the secondary substitutes had already been spoken for.

Upon hearing that, Gene then told her to get an elementary substitute for himself, instead. He then hurried to his school to prepare lesson plans for his substitute, and then rushed over to my school to cover my classes for me that day. He didn't hem or haw. He didn't complain. He never did say, "You owe me." He simply did it! That act so much characterized his life. He simply was like that!

I confess, I had often wondered if life would have been easier for me if I had never married, because then, I would never have known the difference in having to do for myself, or depending upon a spouse to do for me in times of need. If I had never married, then having to do for myself would have become second nature over the years, as opposed to depending upon another source of strength. I would never have known the sweet from the bitter.

Gene had kept me on a pedestal and had treated me like a queen. It had been a difficult adjustment having to do everything myself, having no one to count on but myself, and having no one to do things with anymore.

The telephone had become silent most of the time, which would have been unusual if Gene were still here. It wasn't that he got most of the calls, it was because people stopped calling me because, suddenly, I had changed. I would come home from work, daily, to find no one had phoned that day—not even a salesman! One day, while I was at work, I called my answering machine, just so I would have a message when I arrived home. My drivel went something like this: "Gee, I can't wait to get home to hear what I have to say."

Even the mail was different. It was addressed to only me. Seeing my lone name on the envelopes was a constant reminder of the emptiness I felt. Not even the word "Mrs." was added to my name anymore, as if people thought I was no longer deserving of the title. Perhaps it was because if people wrote it, they might feel they were hurting my feelings. Nevertheless, it made me feel like a nonentity.

One of the hardest things about being suddenly single was the financial aspect. Having total income cut by two-thirds really hurt. I had been used to purchasing nearly anything I had wanted, just about whenever I had wanted. Of course, this blessing had come later in life. I had been fortunate to have been able to stay at home with our growing children, and had only been teaching for eight years prior to Gene's death. Quite suddenly, I was on a very strict, fixed income.

For the first time in my life I was having to carefully budget to make ends meet. It was a bit frightening to realize I was the sole responsible party for all monthly bills. Expenses hadn't changed, only the income to deal with them had changed. There would be no one around to bail me out if I miscalculated my checkbook, as Gene had had to do a couple of times in the past. When I was out of money, there was no other source of income until the next payday.

Paying for my own entertainment was something I had never had to do before. Next to being alone, finances were the hardest things to have to deal with.

One day I read in the paper an announcement for the annual storytellers' conference to be held in Orem. This was an event Gene and I had often attended. One of Gene's many goals was to become involved as a certified national storyteller. The stories he wrote were wonderful, and those who heard his stories were enraptured. He could make up complete plots at the drop of a hat, limited only by the number of hours in a day. Ideas for hundreds of stories were written on scraps of paper I found while cleaning out his desk at home.

Gene's birthday was interesting. I had forgotten about it until flowers were delivered to my classroom. The card was from my daughter. She wished me joy, knowing how hard the day would be for me. Then, remembering it was Gene's birthday, I felt remorseful.

I thought Christmas was going to be disastrous that first year, so I braced for the worst, emotionally. But, it wasn't. There were times when melancholia set in, but it didn't last for long.

Our kids helped me pick out a tree and decorate it. That night I was awakened at 1:30 A.M. by a loud crash. The tree, which had been so meticulously decorated, had fallen over. It was a heavy tree, and I had quite a time trying to heave it up onto the nearby reclining chair so that I could mop up the water from the carpet and toss the tree skirt into the clothes dryer.

As I picked up all the ornaments and glued some of the broken ones back together in the middle of the night, it was then that the tears flowed. I was angry, not that the tree had fallen over, but that Gene hadn't been there to help me clean it up. The following day, my children had to help me upright the tree again and redecorate it.

A few days later, I had a Relief Society meeting at my house. After it was over, and everyone had returned home, I sat in the beauty of my decorated living room. The flickering flames from the fireplace combined with the Christmas tree lights to cast a warm, cozy glow all about me, and the soft Christmas music playing on the CD wrapped up a perfect picture. I sat basking in the beauty of the sights and sounds of the season when, unexpectedly, the tears flowed effortlessly down my cheeks. I missed Gene tremendously the rest of the evening and all the next day.

The morning of the last day of school prior to the winter break, I awoke before my alarm went off. I felt completely rested, peaceful, unusually happy, and eager to take on the day. That feeling of serenity and happiness remained with me throughout the rest of the holiday season.

I had the blessing of family and friends around me all Christmas day, which helped to prevent loneliness.

Eventually, the time came for me to remove the fire hazard (tree) out of the house. I collected all the boxes and organized the task ahead of me. I tackled the tree first. As I removed the ornaments, one-by-one, each bauble brought back memories of Christmases past. As each ornament was carefully packed away into its proper place, my heart felt as though it were being packed away, as well.

I stepped back to view the barren tree and felt extremely saddened that it had been stripped of its beauty, its dignity, and its unique charm. What had only, such a short time before, stood so magnificently, and had given me so much delight, was now barren and dead. It reminded me of Gene. He was so tall and strong, and so full of life one minute, and had brought me so much joy by his simple beauty, but had been stripped of life after such a short season, being as dead as that tree. Undecorating, after the season was over, was the hardest part of Christmas.

Some neighborhood girls had brought me a small, potted, live evergreen tree a few days before Christmas. They'll never understand the significance of that sweet gesture. For, as my Christmas tree was laid to rest in the Christmas tree graveyard, and just as my husband was laid to rest in his own graveyard, that little living evergreen tree reminded me of new life, new hope, new gladness, and life beyond the grave. That little evergreen tree reminded me that Gene's spirit is very much alive and prospering and growing in a realm beyond my mortal vision, just as surely as that little tree was doing the same. Life goes on, which I realized more every day.

February brought the annual Sweethearts Ball to our stake. My Sweetheart and dancing partner wasn't available that year. Another realization struck: I wouldn't be attending any more dances.

It was also income tax season. Gene had prepared tax returns for a clientele he had built over the years. For years, his services included traveling to the clients' homes to prepare their tax information. I always hated the fact that Gene would be away from home night after night for three to four months. However, with our youngest being married, it freed up a bedroom, which was cleverly turned into a professional office for my husband.

Tax clients began coming to our house for income tax preparations, instead of the other way around. I loved this! Although Gene was busy in his office for hours on end, he was still home! Just knowing he was home brought much comfort to me. But now, he wasn't home anymore, and I had to have someone else prepare my taxes.

As the snow fell, it was interesting to me that white sym-
bolizes cleanliness. But, as I looked through my windows at
the snow, I saw how dirty they had become. I had been able
to clean the insides of the windows, but with a two-story
home, I hadn't been able to clean the outsides. Gene had
always cleaned them for me. There was a way they could be
removed from the inside for cleaning. I hadn't yet figured out
how, besides which, they were awkward and, I was sure, too
heavy for me to handle. So I hadn't cleaned them, and they
were desperately dirty.

CHAPTER SIX

A year had gone by since Gene's passing. That first year of transition had been the most difficult, because everything that happened, every day, reminded me of my tremendous loss. I suppose I would never understand, at least in this life, why someone who had been so vital, so consumed with life, and was such a power for good in the lives of so many people, had to be taken, while someone like Hitler, who so adversely affected the lives of millions, was allowed to live for so long.

By then, my receptiveness to the Spirit had diminished somewhat, in that Gene's spirit no longer communicated with mine, as it did those first few months. I missed the sweet comfort it had brought into my life. I could only imagine that it was time for both of us to move forward. Instead of devoting my life to my husband, I needed to devote my life to the Lord and to others now.

Gene had been my entertainer, as well as my greatest fan. My audience had departed, and Gene's stage had been left empty.

In my reading, I finally found the answer for that which I had been seeking these many months. It was right there, in the

Doctrine and Covenants, all along. In section 42, verse 48, it states: "He that hath faith in me to be healed, *and is not appointed unto death,* shall be healed," (Italics added).

President Spencer W. Kimball expounded upon this by explaining, "If one is not appointed unto death, and if sufficient faith is developed, life can be spared. It is evident that even the righteous will not always be healed, and even those of great faith will die when it is according to the purpose of God," ("Tragedy or Destiny," *Improvement Era,* March 1966:178).

Even though many hundreds of faithful people were fasting and praying for Gene to be healed, even though he was on the prayer rolls of several temples around the country, even though many people of many faiths were holding prayer circles for Gene, he died. It had seemed so futile. I had wondered how someone with such a deep and abiding faith could not have been healed.

The answer had finally come to me: he was appointed unto death. This thought brought me peace of mind. It simply was Gene's time to die.

As I contemplated the Easter season, and the one-year anniversary of Gene's death, I had come to a deeper understanding of the resurrection. I had come to realize that the loss of a life is not the real tragedy. The real tragedy would be the loss of faith. It is through faith that I believe in Christ and in His ultimate sacrifice. It is because of His death and resurrection that I know Gene (and all of us) will be resurrected one day. It is through Jesus' atonement that Gene and I will be reunited again. We must keep the eternal perspective in view.

HEALING

CHAPTER SEVEN

I had planned to write this section on healing following the one on transition. Little did I know that healing was definitely going to be a part of the transition process, as well.

Several months following Gene's death, I experienced my first day of healing. It was a very conscious act. It was only a few days following the experience I had in the temple, and was only three days into the new school year.

Driving home from school, the thought struck me soundly that I was a loveable person, and that I had worth. I didn't need a title or a position to "prove" to myself or to anyone else that I was a valuable person. I didn't need to lose twenty pounds or be ten years younger to be worthy of anyone's admiration. "I am who I am," I declared, "and I am okay." I was happy and upbeat all the way home. I am sure Gene's blessing had something to do with my new attitude.

I had been searching for answers in all the wrong places. Self worth doesn't come from the outside world; it comes from within. It doesn't have to be proven. It doesn't have to receive approval from anyone else. It doesn't come with fanfare and banners declaring that one has finally "arrived." It doesn't come in a paycheck. It doesn't come after losing weight or having a face lift. It doesn't come to only the young and beautiful. Self worth is only realized from within. It finally comes after admitting to oneself, and believing it, that you are a worthwhile person by virtue of the fact that you are a child of God.

I realized that day that God loved me the way I was, and was pleased with the way I had been struggling to overcome my trials and was working to keep the commandments. I consciously realized that this was my first day of healing. Just as a deep wound is finally rid of infection and begins to seal together, a physician might say, "Now you are beginning to heal. Soon the pain will diminish, and only a scar will bear the evidence that anything ever happened."

So it is with a deep emotional wound. When the poison of self-pity and defeat is finally gone, healing begins. The pain will slowly diminish, leaving only the scar behind.

The tenth month marked another turning point for me. Quite suddenly, my mind was flooded with the assurance that I could live alone—not that I would enjoy it, especially. Truly, I hated not having my compatriot around! But I knew I could go on. I knew I could face each day and each night with no one but myself for company. I could literally feel myself healing physically, emotionally, and spiritually. I knew that having to go to work each day would not be the dreaded drudgery it had been. I knew my life would go on and that I could be happy.

The answer to a major problem came to me one night in my petition to my Heavenly Father. Since I had never had to be too frugal with money, learning to live on a small, fixed income was crucial.

What seemed to work for me was an idea that came into

my mind during prayer. First, I had my utility companies compute my bills on a fixed monthly rate. Then I made a list of all my regular monthly bills for which I wrote out checks.

Then I made a list of all my expenses which vacillated greatly. For example, although I have my hair cut every six weeks, I needed to save a certain amount each month toward that expense. I would also have to save monthly a specific amount toward expenses such as property taxes on my home and car, as well as insurance for both. I would also have to budget for gasoline and car upkeep, groceries, gifts, dog grooming, entertainment, savings, etc.

On pay day I would go to the bank and deposit into a special account the money I would need from my vacillating list. Into another account I kept the balance of my paycheck, from which I wrote my fixed monthly checks. I knew if I kept all the money in one account, I would spend it.

Another major hurdle for which I needed to find a solution was the constraints upon my time, which had so suddenly been placed upon me. I had been among those who had erroneously thought that anyone living alone had more time than anyone else, because they didn't have to account to anyone but themselves. I learned differently! Living alone meant there was less time. The tasks to be done were not fewer, but the number of hands to tackle them were fewer. The same amount of yard work, house work, repairs, and so forth, had to be done, but now there was no division of labor. I had to do it all, and in the same twenty-four hours a day.

Is it any wonder that statistics show that those who live alone have a shorter life expectancy than those who are married? Perhaps it is because they literally work themselves to death. I had never realized that so dramatically before.

Suddenly, I was left with all the house work, all the laundry, all the yard work, preparing all the meals, doing all the dishes, going to work full-time, doing Church work, and taking charge of after school assignments. There was no one to unload on nor to help me out.

I felt I was treading water in a sea of responsibilities, and I was becoming weary. I was drowning in the murky brine of responsibilities dictated by everything and everybody controlling my time, but me.

Again, I was led through prayer, to a solution which worked for me. I made a list of what I would love to do after work every day if there were no other constraints upon my time. I predicted how long it would take to do each one. The simple pleasures I craved and needed were unattainable up to that time. I wanted to come home from work, read the newspaper and the mail, exercise, read the scriptures, and read something fun—just for me. I figured that all of it would take one and a half hours a day. I decided my peace of mind was worth that.

When I came home from school I would leave phone calls to return after supper. I would allow the answering machine to do its job in that hour and a half. That precious time was mine to sit in the sun, read, unwind, and relax. All the other cares of the day could then be handled afterwards, and with more serenity, because I had taken care of my needs first. It was amazing how much more I seemed to be able to accomplish, and without the resentment.

Of course, every day wasn't ideal, but that was okay. On those hectic days, I would choose only one or two of the things I wanted to do, just as long as I did something each day just for me.

I worked out a schedule to help me account for my time.

On Mondays I would clean the bathrooms. On Tuesdays I would clean the basement level. On Wednesdays I would clean the upstairs level. Thursdays I would do the same for the main level. On Fridays I would clean my kitchen and deck area. Saturdays would be set aside for laundry and for me.

I divided the yard work up into fifths. Each day, as weather permitted, I would put on my back brace and weed and care for one-fifth of my yard. I also found it was to my benefit to hire a yard service to mow and trim the yard weekly.

If something came up in my schedule which prevented me from my daily tasks, I didn't become stressed about it. Neither did I try to make up for it the following day. I simply did the task the following week. I became more mellow, more patient, and less frustrated about all aspects of my life.

Once a week, usually on Saturday, time was set aside to do something special for myself. I could luxuriate in a bubble bath, with scented candles and soft music. I could watch an old movie, or go for a massage. I scheduled "time out" for me, just as I scheduled the mundane things which had to be done.

I learned to take field trips with myself: going to the zoo, taking a long walk, visiting a museum, escaping to a matinee, digging in the garden, sitting in the park, attending a play, listening to the symphony, or going to the beach. I learned to like my own company. I learned I had to nurture myself. I learned to laugh again. I learned I could love again.

Another vexing problem had to do with developing a new support base. I had done everything with my best friend, my husband. Practically every moment we weren't at work, we were together. When Gene died, I felt alone and isolated.

There was no one with whom to travel, or to share my grief or joy—no one with whom to discover things, or to discuss spiritual ideas—no one with whom to take classes, or to share concerns—no one with whom to grow, or to energize me.

I got myself a spiral notebook, and when I had the time, I jotted down topics which brought me solace. Later, when the notebook was filled, I could look back upon each page for comfort and support. Just putting it together was therapy for the soul.

Some of the topics I included were "What I Miss About Gene," "Things I Am Thankful For," "Things I Don't Like," "Activities Which Would Bring Me Pleasure," "Things I Do Like," "All The Friends I Have," "Qualities I Would Require of a New Husband," "What I Like About Myself," "My Favorite Scriptures," etc. It could include any topic of interest to me and could continually be added to and reflected upon.

When acquaintances would ask me how I was doing, sometimes I would have to fib and respond, "I'm doing well," because I believed the more I said it, the more I would incorporate that well-being into my life.

I learned that priesthood blessings can come from any worthy source, not just my husband. I didn't like going elsewhere, but that is the way with life. I have grudgingly had to learn there are resources other than my husband.

I marveled whenever I thought of all the accomplishments credited to Gene's life. He accomplished more in 53 short years than anyone else would have been able to accomplish in twice the time. He earned his Bachelor's Degree in three years, and his Master's Degree in one year, graduating Cum Laude, working full-time, and raising a family. He served a two and a half year mission and learned to speak Spanish fluently. He ran for state legislature, served as a city councilman, spoke at funerals, worked on executive boards, wrote poetry, wrote children's stories, sang in a choir, read dozens of books a year, mostly non-fiction, dabbled in painting, golfed, walked, biked, fished, studied the scriptures regularly, held trustworthy Church callings, spent hours preparing weekly Gospel Doctrine lessons, helped me with house work, yard work, laundry, and cooking. He loved to swim and loved to be in nature. He took time to play with our dog every day. He held a full-time job. He prepared income taxes. He traveled. He even found the time to watch a little television, just to relax. He was well organized and totally committed to everything he did.

He had no bad habits, not even throwing dirty socks on the floor. He was innately patient with our children. He never, never raised his voice to me. He often would bring me flowers for no reason. He never swore. He was powerfully influential in the lives of his family, his students, and his community. He was highly respected among his colleagues. Whatever needed to be done, he was the first to volunteer. Whatever I needed him to do was done immediately; I never had to ask twice.

To this day, even living with him, I cannot understand how he was able to accomplish so much. He had only twenty-four hours a day, the same as I, so why the difference?

During the last four years of Gene's life, I think he felt a real urgency to live each minute to the fullest. Often I would awaken at night to find him in his office working out problems, or he would be sitting up in bed writing stories, or he would be in the living room reading a book in his easy chair. He felt sleep was a real waste of time and often expressed frustration at having to shut down at night.

He was never one to sleep-in or take naps. It was almost

as if Gene knew his time on earth was going to be short. He finally verbalized this to me a few months before his death, but I fluffed it off as only a dream. I regretted that later, because, in retrospect, I was able to see a pattern to his activities leading up to the time of his passing.

At a regional conference in Anchorage, Alaska in 1995, President Gordon B. Hinckley stated,

> I am satisfied that happiness in marriage is not so much a matter of romance as it is an anxious concern for the comfort and well-being of one's companion. Any man who will make his wife's comfort his first concern will stay in love with her throughout their lives and through the eternity yet to come (*Ensign,* Apr. 96:72).

This certainly personified Gene.

He bought me some furniture and appliances to make my life easier, although they were really unneeded. He bought a lawn mower which was easy to start and easy to handle, although the one we had was fairly new, but hard for me to handle. He bought a snow blower. He brought home his personal computer from his classroom at school and set it up for me to use at home. He bought me a new sewing machine. He made sure the house was paid for and that the bills were paid. He had a living trust prepared, as well as a living will. We bought cemetery property. His life was completely in order.

Gene gave me everything in his physical power while he lived. But, he loved me so much, he gave his life for me, so that I would feel compelled to develop a burning testimony of my own. I could no longer depend on Gene for my spiritual welfare. By his dying, I have developed a tremendous desire to attain Celestial life, and I believe, for the first time in my life, that I am capable of attaining that blessing.

This reminded me of my older brother, Jesus, who gave His life for me, preparing the way for me to attain Celestial life. I have grown more, spiritually, in the year following Gene's death than I had in the previous five decades.

I have learned that my Heavenly Father is real, and that He knows who I am, and that He loves me. The reasons have mounted daily as to why my life must go on. I bask in the love of my Heavenly Father. He is my light, my hope, my strength, and my salvation.

Today I have no one to say "Good morning" to, except the Lord. There is no one to say "Good night" to, except the Lord. The companion I walked with is no longer here, so I have learned I must walk with the Lord. No one is here to talk with anymore, so I have learned to talk with the Lord. No one is here for me to depend on anymore, so I have learned I must depend on the Lord. He will sustain me in my needs and in my trials.

My companion is no longer here to hold my hand or to lean on anymore, so I have learned to cast my burdens upon the Lord. No one is here to put his arms around me, to hold me, to love me, or to comfort me, anymore. But the Lord has enfolded me in His love and has given me both comfort and guidance.

For the first time in my life, I have come to depend upon the Lord completely for my very life, my support, my well-being, and my strength. I have found I want to know my Heavenly Father more than I have known Him. I want to serve Him more valiantly than I have served Him. My prayers are more meaningful and more from the heart. My physical body is learning to yield to the longings of my spirit. My spirit has become very tender and forgiving. I am realizing I have worth as a daughter of a Heavenly Father who loves me, and He has witnessed that love to me so many, many times in that first, difficult year.

I came to realize the depth of my belief in the Atonement and Resurrection would measure the degree to which I could be healed. I realized my shattered heart could be healed, and my life could again have meaning.

The basis of this hope was in understanding I had to depend on the Lord for my solace and my strength. To be steadfast in my faith allowed me to receive a healing balm to my broken spirit

I also came to realize that positive emotions provided a buffer against the day-to-day grind. I even resorted to placing signs around my house reminding me to smile, to walk tall, to be happy. I learned to absolve toxic attitudes such as anger, impatience, and whining. After a while, my new attitudes became habits, and I no longer needed the reminders. I felt better, looked happy, was happy, and had more charity toward others.

Life became beautiful again. Joy had returned.

Part One

MOVING ON

CHAPTER EIGHT

My bishop gave me a copy of a quotation from President Ezra Taft Benson entitled "A Promise." It became my daily guide:

> Men and women who turn their lives to God will find out that He can make a lot more of their lives than they can. He will deepen their joys, expand their vision, quicken their minds, strengthen their muscles, lift their spirits, multiply their blessings, increase their opportunities, comfort their souls, raise up friends, and pour out peace. Whoever will lose his life to God will find he has eternal life (*Teachings of Ezra Taft Benson,* Bookcraft:Salt Lake City, p.361).

What greater promise could I have to live by than this? I can testify that it works in my life.

I'm thankful for a surety of life in the hereafter and of the great and marvelous work taking place in the Spirit World. I'm thankful the Lord had faith in my husband to participate in such rich and rewarding work. I'm thankful the Lord had faith in me to carry on in this life without my eternal companion.

Nearly everyone loves a story with a happy ending, but happiness can be defined in a hundred different ways by a hundred different persons. So, I'll let the reader write his or her own ending to this story. Suffice it to say that, according to my standard of happiness, all is well with me, as I have learned to live again, and to be happy again.

I can see farther into eternity

because I have been lifted up by

the arms of a gentle giant.

A B O U T   T H E   A U T H O R

Patty Rosvall, ADN, BS, is currently a biology teacher in Salt Lake County. She is a member of Utah Speakers Association and owns her own company, New Beginnings, which special-izes in helping others to realize his or her individual worth.

The experience of losing her husband of twenty five years, and the ensuing growth and strength she developed, led to her desire to motivate others to achieve personal change and restore emotional healing in their lives.